International Biographies

Book 1
Africa and the Middle East

Mary Anne Anderson

Stephanie M. Hamilton

Karen Martin Tryda

Mary Anne Anderson earned her M.Ed. in curriculum and instruction at Kent State University, Kent, Ohio. She is a language arts teacher and reading specialist. She has over ten years of experience at elementary and middle school levels.

Stephanie M. Hamilton earned her B.S. in education at Bowling Green State University, Bowling Green, Ohio. A college English teacher and student life counselor, she has also taught at the elementary level and has published articles in *Early Years* and in *Highlights for Children.*

Karen Martin Tryda, who earned her M.Ed. in curriculum and instruction at Cleveland State University, Cleveland, Ohio, has received national acclaim as an elementary social studies teacher. She is the author of numerous articles and curriculum units, including Intermediate Social Studies *World History and Geography Books 1* and *2*, published by The Center for Learning.

The Publishing Team

Rose Schaffer, M.A., Executive Director
Bernadette Vetter, M.A., Associate Director
Diane Podnar, M.S., Production Director
Lora Murphy, M.A., Curriculum Director

Cover design and illustrations
Reed Simon

Series Editor
Victoria Palisin

List of credits found on Acknowledgments Page beginning on page 145.

ISBN 1-56077-192-5

Contents

Appendix

Preface

The *International Biographies Series* is an active exploration and description of the lives of ninety-eight people who have affected the course of world history.

Supported by centuries of acquired facts, anecdotes, and legends, and mindful of the need for reform advocated by groups such as the Bradley Commission and the National Commission on Social Studies in the Schools, a team of Center for Learning teacher-authors determined to revolutionize the traditional approach to humanities in the classroom.

They were governed by a single cause—the development of new multicultural curriculum units which would offer an unparalleled *living* record of the story of our humankind.

Sustained by the certainty that people are interested in people, the teachers selected for biographical study a rich diversity of historical figures, the well-known and not-so-famous, men and women of varied races, creeds, and heritages—all contributors to development of world cultures.

The team outlined, organized, defined, researched, clarified, emphasized, wrote, edited, rewrote, and unified until parts turned whole and history became human.

The process proved that history is **not** dull. The outcome, seven curriculum units, is a unique circling of the globe narrating singular, individual achievements, a relevant linking of North, South, East, and West in a practical design that will inspire the young to understand the old world and the new . . . and to enjoy the discovery!

Distinguishing Features of the Series

- Supports universal, core *values* vital to America and the world
- *Empowers teachers* by modeling a creative, active instructional approach
- Maintains a *student-centered, active* approach to learning
- Features *brief biographies* written in a *lively narrative* style with emphasis on *human interest* aspects of persons' lives
- Creates learning situations in which a *wide range of abilities* can function
- Improves student *self-image* by demonstrating that each person can make a difference
- Presents a *positive, upbeat* story of the world while maintaining *historical accuracy*

Introduction

At whatever K–12 level the humanities are taught, the interdisciplinary units of the *International Biographies Series* are a natural supplement. Each lesson is self-contained and designed to be teacher-tailored to a broad range of student audiences. The abundance of hands-on activities, a distinguishing characteristic of this series, inspires student participation at individual and diverse levels of experience.

Emphasizing an active and creative instructional approach, the cross-disciplinary units interweave English/language arts, mathematics, science, music, art, and other disciplines with the organizing strand of social studies content. Although history and geography predominate, economics, political science, sociology, and other areas of social studies are included.

The books of the series are ordered alphabetically by continent or geographic area. The fourteen biographies within each book are presented in alphabetical order and cover from ancient to modern times.

This instructional material complements the graded courses of study, K–12 scope and sequence models, and frameworks developed by state and school districts.

International Biographies Series

Book 1—Africa and the Middle East

1. Cleopatra
2. Kahlil Gibran
3. Jomo Kenyatta
4. Lawrence of Arabia
5. Miriam Makeba
6. Makeda: Queen of Sheba
7. Nelson Mandela
8. Mansa Musa
9. Queen Nefertiti
10. Julius Nyerere
11. Alan Paton
12. Anwar Sadat
13. Haile Selassie
14. Shaka Zulu

Book 2—Asia, Australia, and Oceania

1. Corazon Aquino
2. Matsuo Bashō
3. Buddha
4. Indira Gandhi
5. Evonne Goolagong
6. Hammurabi
7. Hirohito
8. Genghis Khan
9. Kublai Khan
10. Queen Liliuokalani
11. Kiri Te Kanawa
12. Mother Teresa
13. U Thant
14. Mao Zedong

Book 3—Europe
(Central and Southern)

1. Otto von Bismarck
2. Charlemagne
3. Jacques Cousteau
4. Charles de Gaulle
5. Gustave Eiffel
6. Albert Einstein
7. Joan of Arc
8. Martin Luther
9. Michelangelo
10. Napoleon
11. Nostradamus
12. Pablo Picasso
13. Marco Polo
14. Wernher Von Braun

Book 4—Europe
(Eastern)

1. Alexander the Great
2. Kemal Mustapha Ataturk
3. Attila the Hun
4. Catherine the Great
5. Marie Curie
6. Peter Carl Fabergé
7. Mikhail Gorbachev
8. Wolfgang Amadeus Mozart
9. Nicholas II
10. Sappho
11. Joseph Stalin
12. Peter Ilyich Tchaikovsky
13. Valentina Tereshkova
14. Tito

Book 5—Europe
(Northern and Western)

1. Hans Christian Andersen
2. Charles Dickens
3. Leif Ericson
4. Sonja Henie
5. Henry VIII
6. Mary Kingsley
7. Rudyard Kipling
8. Florence Nightingale
9. Alfred B. Nobel
10. Beatrix Potter
11. Lionel de Rothschild
12. William Shakespeare
13. Margaret Thatcher
14. Queen Victoria

Book 6—Latin America
(Central and South)

1. Salvador Allende
2. Atahualpa
3. Balboa
4. Simón Bolívar
5. Fidel Castro
6. Roberto Clemente
7. Christopher Columbus
8. Maximilian
9. Gabriela Mistral
10. Montezuma
11. Pelé
12. Eva Perón
13. Martin de Porres
14. Diego Rivera

Book 7—North America
(U.S. and Canada)

1. Big Bear
2. Aaron Copland
3. Walt Disney
4. Matthew Henson
5. Henry Hudson
6. N. Scott Momaday
7. Grandma Moses
8. Annie Oakley
9. Bobby Orr
10. Theodore Roosevelt
11. Robert Service
12. Sam Steele
13. Pierre Trudeau
14. James Van DerZee

Teacher Notes

Lesson Title – Same heading that appears on contents page and at the beginning of the lesson
Featured Activities – Specific student functions
Area of Achievement – Role(s) of the person being studied
Geographic Themes – NCGE's geographic themes from *Guidelines for Geographic Education: Elementary and Secondary Schools* which the lesson addresses
Objectives – Desired student outcomes
Skills – List of skills which the lesson reinforces
Interdisciplinary Strands – Disciplines involved

Teacher Sections

The first pages of each lesson are written exclusively for the teacher. They contain the following information:
Objectives – Never more than three and always student-centered
Interdisciplinary Strands – Specific subject areas interwoven in the lesson
Notes to the Teacher – Background information and lesson overview
Materials – List of the items needed to teach the lesson as written
Terms – Vocabulary with which students need to be familiar
Sources – Some useful resources; check the local/school libraries for others
Procedures – A step-by-step suggested teaching approach
Enrichment /Extension – Optional activities for follow-up
Art Notation – Explanation of portraits

Student Materials

The last few pages of each lesson are activity sheets to be reproduced for students. They are of two types:
Samples—Examples provided for guidance; these pages are used to link the individual activity with specific content keyed to the person being studied.
Handouts—Templates to be used for student work; these can be collected, kept in portfolio, and later combined to form a student-written book.

Tips for Using the Unit

Necessary instructions appear under the procedures in the teacher's section or on the student handout. Answers to handouts will vary unless otherwise indicated.

A *culminating product*—A resource book which is completely student-written material—is a viable option. The templates are designed to make this possible.

Each lesson is self-contained and designed to be *teacher-adapted.* The unit, in whole or part, can be adapted to whole language or traditional settings.

Suggested *assignments* provide both classwork and homework. Students are asked to complete activities outside of class time, but they are also provided with opportunities for classwork where the teacher and their peers are available as resources.

The use of the *library*—and other beyond-the-classroom resources (family, friends, neighborhood, community) are *utilized.*

There is a broad array of *skills* inherent in the lessons ranging from lower-level information retrieval to higher-level decision making and critical thinking.

The *illustrations* provide an opportunity to reinforce critical thinking skills and enhance self-expression. See Appendix, **Handout 58.**

The unit lends itself to a *group-work* format. Consider it as an option even in lessons where it is not specifically suggested.

The overall approach is *student-centered* and active rather than passive. The role of the teacher is to be a facilitator and guide . . . a supporting actor, not the star. Encourage students to help one another and themselves.

Cross Reference Chart

	Lesson Title	Featured Activities	Area of Achievement	Geography Themes
1.	Cleopatra (69–30 B.C.)	Creating an Egyptian god or goddess	Political Leader	Location Place Movement Region
2.	Kahlil Gibran (1883–1931)	Interpreting wise sayings Making a philosophy cube	Writer	Location Place Movement Regions
3.	Jomo Kenyatta (1889?–1978)	Playing an African game Designing a personal symbol	Political Leader	Location Place
4.	Lawrence of Arabia (1888–1935)	Designing a family crest	Political Leader	Location Place Regions
5.	Miriam Makeba (1932–)	Creating a necklace	Muscian, Political Leader	Location Place

Cross Reference Chart

Objectives	Skills	Interdisciplinary Strands
To identify Cleopatra as a queen of ancient Egypt To examine pictures of ancient Egyptian gods and goddesses To create a god or goddess	Brainstorming Locating Reading Discussing Retelling Examining Symbolizing Creating/Drawing Writing	Art English/Language Arts Geography History Religion
To identify Kahlil Gibran as a Middle Eastern philosopher, writer, and painter To interpret several of Gilbran's wise sayings and stories To make a philosophy cube	Discussing Webbing Brainstorming Locating Reading Sharing Interpreting Writing Constructing Decorating	Art English/Language Arts Geography History Philosophy
To identify Jomo Kenyatta as a leader in Kenya's fight for independence To recognize the importance of symbols and to create personal symbols	Game playing Counting Examining Locating Reading Discussing Comparing Creating Symbolizing Writing	Art English/Language Arts Geography History
To identify the role of T.E. Lawrence in gaining Arab independence To examine a crest designed for Lawrence of Arabia To design a family crest	Discussing Visualizing Locating Reading Examining Symbolizing Designing	Art English/Language Arts Geography History
To identify Miriam Makeba as a South African singer and political activist To recognize the influence an entertainer has on world opinion To create a necklace symbolizing your homeland	Listening Locating Discussing Reading Sharing Hypothesizing Examining Designing Crafting	Art English/Language Arts Geography History Music

Cross Reference Chart

	Lesson Title	Featured Activities	Area of Achievement	Geography Themes
6.	Makeda: Queen of Sheba (10th century B.C.)	Charting a trade route	Political Leader	Location Place Movement Regions
7.	Nelson Mandela (1918–)	Creating a collage	Political Leader, Social Reformer	Location Place
8.	Mansa Musa (? –1337)	Designing a trade caravan	Political Leader	Location Place Human-Environment Interaction Movement
9.	Queen Nefertiti (1388?–1349BC)	Making a personal qualities list	Political Leader	Location Place
10.	Julius Nyerere (1922–)	Creating an illustrated map of Tanzania	Political Leader	Location Place Human-Environment Interaction

Cross Reference Chart

Objectives	Skills	Interdisciplinary Strands
To identify Makeda, the Queen of Sheba, as a ruler of Ancient Arabia To discover the geography and trade routes of the empire of Sheba To chart a trade route between North American cities	Questioning Discussing Reading Locating Map Reading Sharing Charting	Economics English/Language Arts Geography History
To identify Nelson Mandela as a leader in the fight against apartheid in South Africa To create a collage depicting key ideas and events in Mandela's life	Discussing Locating Reading Charting Planning Designing/Arranging Writing	Art English/Language Arts Geography History
To identify Mansa Musa as an emperor of the ancient African kingdom of Mali To explore the importance of trade to the people of Mali To design a trade caravan	Trading Sharing Communicating Discussing Reading Map Reading Locating Examining Drawing/Designing	Art Economics English/Language Arts Geography History
To recognize Queen Nefertiti as a queen of ancient Egypt To identify characteristics of Queen Nefertiti To recognize and list personal qualities unique to each student	Examining Discussing Reading Locating Describing Calculating Writing	Art English/Language Arts Geography History Math
To identify Julius Nyerere and his contributions to the independence of Tanzania To create an illustrated map of Tanzania	Counting (in Swahili) Discussing Locating Reading Examining Map Reading Drawing Presenting	Art English/Language Arts Geography History

Cross Reference Chart

	Lesson Title	Featured Activities	Area of Achievement	Geography Themes
11.	Alan Paton (1903–1988)	Producing a slogan	Social Reformer, Writer	Location Place Regions
12.	Anwar Sadat (1918–1981)	Role-playing making a decision	Political Leader	Location Place Movement Regions
13.	Haile Selassie (1892–1975)	Creating a banner	Political Leader	Location Place Human-Environment Interaction
14.	Shaka Zulu (1787–1829)	Making a comic strip	Political Leader	Location

Cross Reference Chart

Objectives	Skills	Interdisciplinary Strands
To identify Alan Paton and his role in the fight against apartheid in South Africa To produce a slogan to protest social injustice	Examining Discussing Researching Locating Reading Sharing Listing Writing Designing	Art English/Language Arts Geography History Literature
To identify Anwar Sadat as a leader of Egypt and a peacemaker in the Middle East To examine the decision-making process To role play making decisions	Discussing Reading Locating Describing Brainstorming Sharing Decision-making Writing Role-playing	Drama English/Language Arts Geography History Political Science
To identify Haile Selassie as Ethiopia's last emperor To create a commemorative symbol of Selassie's rule	Writing Discussing Reading Locating Comparing Drawing Symbolizing Designing	Art English/Language Arts Geography History Political Science
To identify the contributions of Shaka Zulu as an African tribal chief To make a comic strip depicting an event in Shaka's life	Discussing Locating Reading Examining Sequencing Designing Writing	Art English/Language Arts Geography History Political Science

Cleopatra

Objectives

- To identify Cleopatra as a queen of ancient Egypt
- To examine pictures of ancient Egyptian gods and goddesses
- To create a god or goddess

Notes to the Teacher

Cleopatra was a queen of ancient Egypt. In order to understand her story, students need to have some background about the ancient Egyptian Empire. More than 3,000 years before the Christian era, a highly developed civilization flourished along the Nile River in Egypt. It was one of the great powers of the ancient Mediterranean world and retained dominant power for over 2,000 years. During this time, the empire was ruled by a king or queen who was considered to be an incarnation of the god Horus. A system of religion that had many gods and goddesses developed and great tombs or pyramids were built. The Egyptian civilization made great advances in art, mathematics, astronomy, and culture.

Around 1,000 B.C. Egypt entered a long period of decline. By the time Cleopatra and her brother became rulers of Egypt in 51 B.C., Rome had replaced Egypt as the leading power in the Mediterranean world. Cleopatra schemed to become sole ruler and to regain some of the lost glory of Egypt. She used her charm to ally herself with the Roman rulers and to murder in order to rid herself of possible rivals.

Students read a biography of Cleopatra and discuss her desire to rule Egypt and the questionable methods she used to expand her empire. They then examine a part of Egyptian culture, the religious system of gods and goddesses, and create their own version of a god or goddesses.

INTERDISCIPLINARY STRANDS:
Art, English/Language Arts, Geography, History, Religion

MATERIALS:
Handouts 1, **2**, and **3**, markers and crayons, world wall map

TERMS:
ally, barge, conquest, Caesar, empire, venom

Resources

Boase, Wendy. *Ancient Egypt.* New York: Gloucester Press, 1978.
Hoobler, Dorothy and Thomas. *Cleopatra.* New York: Chelsea House Publishers, 1986.
Leighton, Margaret. *Cleopatra: Sister of the Moon.* New York: Farrar, Straus & Giroux, 1969.
Stead, Miriam. *Ancient Egypt.* New York: Gloucester Press, 1985.

Procedure

1. Write the word "Egypt" on the chalkboard. Have students brainstorm any words or phrases that come to mind (possible answers: pyramid, Nile River, pharaohs, country, King Tut, desert, mummies, etc.). Use the portrait at the beginning of **Handout 1** to inspire other ideas.

2. Locate Egypt on a world wall map. Point out that it is in Northern Africa, on the Mediterranean Sea, and the Nile River runs through it. Also locate the cities of Alexandria, Roma, Taurus (in Asia Minor), and Athens.

3. Explain that over 3,000 years before the birth of Christ, Egypt was a great empire that ruled the Mediterranean area. This was when the pyramids were built. After over 2,000 years of Egyptian rule, other countries became more powerful and by 200 B.C. Rome had become the ruling power of the area.

4. If Cleopatra was not mentioned during brainstorming, introduce her now as a famous queen of Egypt. Have students read her biography in **Handout 1** to find out how she became ruler of Egypt.

5. Discuss the biography by having students tell the story of Cleopatra in their own words. Emphasize the idea of her desire to be queen and ruler of a large empire and the methods she used to achieve her goal. *(She used her charms and schemes to ally herself with powerful Roman rulers.)* Also note the unhappy ending to the story. *(She and Marc Anthony took their own lives when they realized they were conquered by Octavian.)* Conclude by discussing if Cleopatra's methods were right and if such methods could be used today.

6. Explain that Egyptian culture included the belief in many gods and goddesses. Distribute **Handout 2**. Examine the pictures and discuss specific characteristics of each god or goddess. Point out that often they were pictured with human bodies and animal heads. Each animal represented specific characteristics. For instance, Sebek, the crocodile god, might make you think of a crafty crocodile patiently waiting for an unsuspecting animal to come near. Sebek could represent patience to some or ferocity and scheming to others.

7. Have students create their own god or goddess using **Handout 3**. Ask them to write a paragraph describing the outstanding characteristic of their god or goddess and explaining why people would pray to them.

8. Display the gods and goddesses in the classroom.

Enrichment/Extension

1. Research the Egyptian gods and goddess. Make sketches and write a paragraph telling what the god or goddess represents and why it was worshipped. Display these next to the gods and goddesses created by the class. (See Appendix, **Handout 45.**)

2. Construct a pyramid of construction paper or other materials. Have the pyramid open to reveal the burial chamber. Include hieroglyphics on the walls and a mummy inside the chamber.

3. Read William Shakespeare's play, *Anthony and Cleopatra* or George Bernard Shaw's *Caesar and Cleopatra.* Compare the literary accounts with the historical account of Cleopatra.

4. Other potential lessons relating to ancient Egypt can be found in "Egyptian Hieroglyphs," *World History and Geography Book 1: The East* (Villa Maria, Pa.: The Center for Learning, 1991).

Art Notation

Cleopatra's portrait depicts her wearing the vulture crown of ancient Egypt. The triangle atop the portrait represents a pyramid, another traditional symbol of Egypt. (See Appendix, **Handout 58**.)

Student Activity
International Biographies
Book 1
Lesson 1, Handout 1 (page 1)
Sample

Name____________________

Date ____________________

Cleopatra

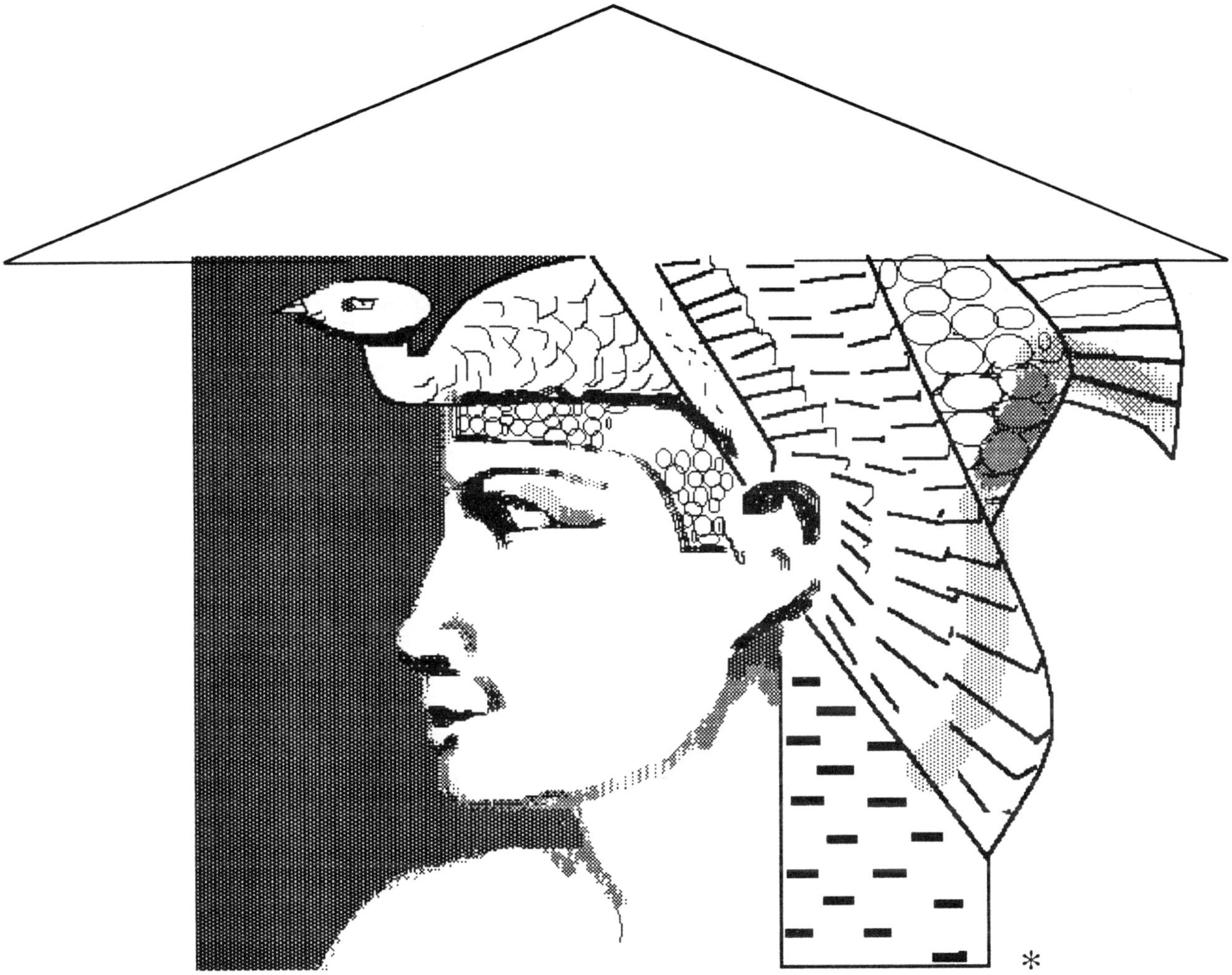

*

Who would rule Egypt . . . Cleopatra or her brother? The decision would be made by the Roman conqueror, Julius Caesar. Cleopatra was determined to get to the city of Alexandria and appeal directly to Caesar. She was a beautiful woman and had charmed many men. She was certain she could charm Caesar. Her brother, Ptolemy, however, was equally determined to prevent Cleopatra from seeing Julius Caesar. His soldiers were instructed to kill Cleopatra when she tried to get into the palace. What could she do?

* The illustration of Cleopatra is based on an artist's representation.

Name________________________

Date ________________________

It was a problem Cleopatra solved in a unique way. She sailed down the Nile River toward Alexandria. As the boat approached the city, knowing she could not walk into the palace unrecognized, she instructed her friends to wrap her in a rug. They carried the folded-up rug (some versions of the story say it was the coverlet of a bed) past the guards and into Caesar's apartment. The party approached Caesar and spread their "gift" before him. As the rug unrolled, Cleopatra appeared. One book says, " . . . she rose up as if in a fairy tale. Caesar was delighted."[1] The charmed Caesar selected Cleopatra and not Ptolemy as ruler of Egypt.

The woman we call Cleopatra was actually Cleopatra VII. She began her reign when she was about eighteen years old, after her father died in 51 B.C. According to Egyptian custom, she married her brother. With Caesar's help she dethroned her brother. Cleopatra was determined to restore Egypt to its former glory and decided that Julius Caesar could help her accomplish her goal.

Caesar spent the winter with Cleopatra, cruising the Nile on her royal barge before resuming his military campaigns. Cleopatra and Caesarion, her son by Caesar, followed him to Rome in 46 B.C. Since the Romans considered other countries and peoples to be inferior, they resented Caesar's attentions to Cleopatra, especially when he placed a statue of her in a Roman temple and settled her into his country home. He also made her a Roman citizen and a member of his own family. On behalf of Caesar's wife, Calpurnia, the Romans were outraged.

Julius Caesar was assassinated in 44 B.C. Three men (Marc Anthony, Octavian, and Marcus Lepidus) joined forces to rule Rome. Cleopatra quickly left Rome and returned to Egypt. She did not trust the Romans. Shortly after her arrival in Alexandria, her husband-brother was killed, many suspected by Cleopatra's orders. Cleopatra ruled as queen. Marc Anthony, one of Rome's rulers after Caesar, summoned her to Tarsus, a city in Asia Minor.

Cleopatra had met Marc Anthony in Rome and thought that he could be an ally. She needed allies. Egypt had many crops but a weak army. She needed someone with a strong army to protect Egypt. She needed to charm Marc Anthony the way she had charmed Caesar so she could secure his military might to keep Egypt safe.

[1]Dorothy and Thomas Hoobler, *Cleopatra,* (New York: Chelsea House, 1986), 40.

Name______________________

Date ______________________

There is no record of what Cleopatra did. However, whatever she did it impressed Marc Anthony, and he soon gave her the island of Cyprus as well as Egypt to rule. Cleopatra arranged to have her one surviving sister killed. She was then the only one with a claim to the throne. She had nothing to fear at home and was free to turn her attention elsewhere.

Anthony and Cleopatra joined a group known as "The Order of Those Who Live for Pleasure." They took turns having elaborate entertainments and feasts. While Anthony and Cleopatra were throwing parties, Octavian, another of the rulers of Rome following the death of Caesar, was plotting against them.

Anthony's wife, Fulvia, died, and Anthony returned to Rome. While there, he and the two other rulers divided the Roman Empire, with Anthony getting the eastern part. As part of the agreement, Anthony married Octavia, Octavian's sister. Marc Anthony remained in Rome and made plans to conquer Parthia and to control his part of the empire. Meanwhile, Cleopatra remained in Egypt.

After three years everything was in readiness and Anthony set off with his army on the Parthian campaign. He sent for Cleopatra when he reached Antioch, Syria, and she went to be with him. He gave her and her children more land, lands that once belonged to Egypt. He also recognized the twins she had borne, Alexander Helios and Cleopatra Selene, as his children. Cleopatra's dream was coming true: the Egyptian Empire was expanding.

When spring came Anthony launched an unsuccessful attack on Parthia. Cleopatra returned to Alexandria and gave birth to another son, Ptolemy Philadelphus. She started to raise money and get supplies as Anthony returned to Alexandria to plan a new campaign. They resumed their former lifestyle. Octavia sent word that she was bringing fresh troops and supplies from Athens. Anthony refused to leave Cleopatra. He took the supplies and troops from Octavia but would not see her. Octavia returned to Rome. Anthony divorced her. Her brother, Octavian, declared war on Egypt.

Octavian's navy defeated Anthony's and Cleopatra's forces off the coast of Greece. Many of Anthony's men deserted to Octavian's army, and many of the rulers of the eastern provinces who had been on Anthony's side also joined Octavian. Anthony and Cleopatra fled to Egypt.

Name____________________

Date ____________________

Despite the situation they were in, Anthony and Cleopatra resumed their pleasurable celebrations again. However, "The Order of Those Who Live for Pleasure" had its name changed to "The Order of Those Inseparable in Death" which indicates that Anthony and Cleopatra felt their days were numbered. In addition, Cleopatra began to test various poisons on condemned prisoners to determine which was fast-acting but painless. Her experiments led her to believe that the venom of the asp, a snake native to Egypt, was the best choice.

Finally, Octavian advanced toward Egypt. Anthony went out with his army to repel the attack. The Egyptian army and navy quickly surrendered. Cleopatra fled to Alexandria. Anthony did not know where she was and thought she was dead. He stabbed himself. He was taken to Cleopatra but died. Cleopatra was taken prisoner by the Romans.

Cleopatra found herself once again in need of an ally. She had charmed Julius Caesar. She had charmed Marc Anthony. Could she now charm Octavian? History records that she tried and failed. When she learned that she was to be taken back to Rome and paraded through the streets as a conquest, she arranged for an asp to be brought to her; some think it was concealed in a basket of figs. She had decided to let the asp bite her and die what she hoped would be a quick and painless death. She was buried beside Marc Anthony, along with her dream of returning Egypt to its former glory.

Name________________________

Date ________________________

Egyptian Gods and Goddesses

The ancient Egyptians had many gods and goddesses. Often they were pictured with human bodies and animals heads. Examine the gods and goddesses below. Think about the characteristics that come to mind when you see their pictures. Why would people pray to these gods?

Hathor (Goddess of love, women, childbirth, and music.)

She had the head of a cow.

Fig 1.1

Horus (King of the Gods)

God of light and heaven. He had the head of a falcon and an ankh in his hand. The ankh symbolized life.

Fig 1.2

Anubis (God of the dead.)

He was the guard of the tombs and pyramids and had the head of a jackal.

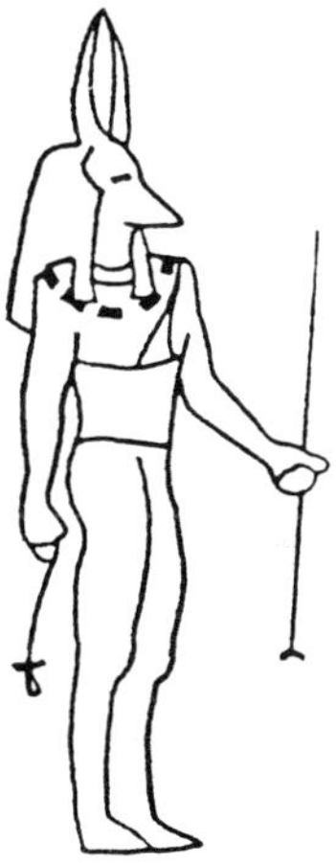

Fig 1.3

Sekhmet (Goddess of war.)

She had the head of a lion.

Fig 1.4

Figs 1.1.–1.4 Adapted from Lorraine Conway, *Ancient Egypt* (Carthage, Ill.: Good Apple Inc., 1987).

Name________________________

Date ________________________

My Egyptian God or Goddess

Kahlil Gibran

Objectives

- To identify Kahlil Gibran as a Middle Eastern philosopher, writer, and painter
- To interpret several of Gibran's wise sayings and stories
- To make a philosophy cube

Notes to the Teacher

This lesson revolves around the life of a philosopher whose ideas are often quite complicated, Kahlil Gibran. Although much of his writing deals directly with religious ideas or has religious overtones, an inappropriate emphasis in a public school, his philosophy reflects views on many other areas of general interest. He brings ideas from Middle Eastern culture to the Western world. The understanding of the culture of the Middle East is especially relevant considering the tensions and turmoil in that area of the world. A brief discussion of current events, problems, and emotions about this region can serve as background to a study of Gibran.

Students read a biography of Gibran. They also read several of his wise sayings and stories, evaluate his ideas, and use critical thinking skills to consider what Gibran is trying to teach with each writing. Students use his ideas to examine their own views of life and what rules they live by. They then write their philosophy of life on a cube for display.

Healthy discussion dealing with social adjustment and the role of the individual in society or the variance in value systems of individuals and groups that is part of cultural diversity can be an outgrowth of this lesson.

INTERDISCIPLINARY STRANDS:
Art, English/Language Arts, Geography, History, Philosophy

MATERIALS:
Handouts 4, **5**, and **6**, scissors, markers, glue or tape, world wall map

TERMS:
Arabic, Christian, Jew, Marionite, Muslim, philosopher, raiment, scholar

Resources

Ferris, Anthony R., Ed. *Kahlil Gibran: A Self Portrait.* New York: The Citadel Press, 1959.
Gibran, Kahlil. *The Treasured Writings of Kahlil Gibran.* New York: Castle Books, a Division of Book Sales, Inc. 1980.
Gibran, Kahlil. *The Wanderer: His Parables and His Sayings.* New York: Alfred A. Knopf, 1971.
Sheban, Joseph, Ed. *The Wisdom of Gibran: Aphorisms and Maxims.* New York: Philosophical Library, 1966.

Procedure

1. Conduct a brief discussion of Operation Desert Storm or current event in the Middle East. Ask if students know of anyone who fought in Operation Desert Storm or who has lived in or visited the Middle East. Make a web on the chalkboard with the Middle East as the starting point. Have students brainstorm their views about people who live in the Middle East. Have them tell what they know about cultures of this region and how well the United States gets along with the various countries there. Why do they think there is tension in this part of the world? *(Answers should include the idea of the difference in cultures as well as the economic significance of rich oil fields.)*

2. Locate the various Middle Eastern countries on a world wall map. Discuss the climate and culture found here. Note the presence of large oil fields and their importance to the world's economy. Also point out that this area is the birthplace of three great religions: Christianity, Islam (Muslim), and Judaism.

3. Locate Lebanon on the map and explain that a great philosopher (a person who studies the meaning of life and right and wrong) was born here. His ideas helped people in the West understand the culture and ideas of the Middle East.

4. Read Kahlil Gibran's biography in **Handout 4**.

5. Discuss his biography and ask why Gibran's writings which helped East understand the West a little better and vice versa makes a difference. Let them discuss this point. Help students understand the parable at the end of the biography.

6. Distribute **Handout 5** and go over the maxims. Divide students into small groups. (See Appendix, **Handout 48**.) Have each group see if they can determine what Gibran meant by each maxim. Encourage them to use a dictionary to find the meaning of unfamiliar words.

7. Reconvene the class and discuss the results of their small group work. Try to get a consensus for each saying.

8. Distribute **Handout 6** along with scissors, markers, glue, or tape. Have students think of some original sayings that reflect their own values or rules about various aspects of life. They can use some of the categories on **Handout 5** or they can add others such as Friendship, Home, Courage, Education, Hope, Family, Love, Hate, Money, Justice, Music, Nature, Patriotism, Self, Truth, Time, etc.

9. Have them write their original sayings, one to a section, on the cube in pen or marker. Encourage them to decorate each section with the markers.

10. Cut out the cube on the solid lines and assemble by folding on the dotted lines. Glue or tape the sections together to form a three-dimensional cube.

11. Display the completed cubes by hanging them by threads individually from ceiling or create several mobiles by hanging the cubes from two yardsticks that have been tied together to form an X-shape. Depending upon the size of the class, more than one set of yardsticks may be needed to display all of the cubes.

Enrichment/Extension

1. Examine quotations made by Benjamin Franklin to see what he had to say about the various "rules" he had about life. Have groups of two or three students present at least one of his sayings in the form of a pantomime to see if the others can guess what the saying is. (Check each group to insure that no saying is repeated.)

2. Examine the geography of Lebanon to see why Gibran loved this country so much. Collect or draw pictures of the cities and the countryside as it was at the turn of the century, including the cedars and cypress trees. Display the pictures within the classroom. Examine the political problems found in Lebanon today and how this affects the way some of the area now looks. Display pictures or drawings of modern Lebanon next to the pictures of turn-of-the-century Lebanon. Compare and contrast the pictures.

3. Read other writings by Kahlil Gibran. Present a report to the class. (See Appendix, **Handout 46**.)

4. Other potential lessons relating to the culture of the Middle East can be found in "Semitic World: Middle East—Arabs, Israelis," *World Cultures and Geography* (Villa Maria, Pa.: Center for Learning, 1987).

Art Notations

Kahlil Gibran's portrait depicts him with the thoughtful expression of a philosopher. His philosophy, so beautifully expressed in his writings, has made him known and loved around the world as represented by the circle. (See Appendix, **Handout 58**.)

Name________________________

Date ________________________

Kahlil Gibran

What is your name? How did you get your name? What would your name be if you had been named for one of your grandparents? Would you have liked that name? In some places children are named for parents or grandparents. It is their tradition. You will meet a man in this story who was named in this way.

Name____________________

Date ____________________

Kahlil Gibran became a famous writer of poems, essays, and stories that are known around the world. He was recognized as a scholar and a philosopher. Through his writing, he helped Middle Eastern countries understand something of the West and European and American countries were able to better understand the ideas of the Middle East. He was a man who loved his fellow man regardless of their religious affiliations. His writings were simple and they told of ideas that he had learned as he went through life. They told of love, happiness, sadness—all of life's emotions. He wrote in Arabic and later in English. His paintings and drawings have also been displayed all over the world. Many consider him a genius.

He studied Arabic and Syriac in the schools where he was born, but when he was about twelve years old, he moved to the United States with his mother and his two sisters and a brother. They settled in Boston, Massachusetts, in 1895.

Gibran was a very shy person who some people thought was strange. Even when he was a little boy, he stayed by himself and read, drew, or played quietly. When he talked with other children, they really did not understand some of the things he said, and they left him alone.

He went to a public school for boys in Boston for about two and a half years. When he left this school, he went to night school for another year. Then he wanted to go home to Lebanon to attend a college called "The School of Wisdom."

When Gibran graduated, he traveled throughout the Middle East. He liked visiting historic sites, but in 1902 he returned to the United States. He was never to return to his beloved Lebanon again.

When he was twenty-five, he went to Paris to study art for three years. His teacher was the famous sculptor who made "The Thinker," Auguste Rodin. Rodin thought that Gibran was going to be a famous artist because he showed so much talent in art and poetry. When he finished his studies, Gibran made his home in New York. Gibran began to write about his feelings and life experiences.

In his writing there is sometimes sadness because he had some very sad things happen to him in his life. His sister, Sultana, died when he was nineteen and he had loved her very much. Then a year later, his only brother, Peter, died. Three months after Peter's death, his mother died.

Name________________________

Date ________________________

He had loved his mother very, very much. He had only his sister Miriana left from his family and he often visited her in her home in Boston, Massachusetts.

Gibran remained a poor man most of his life and lived in a fourth floor New York apartment where he had to walk up and down. His poverty caused him to remain single. He met his first love in Lebanon while he was in college, and he wanted to marry her. Her father, however, refused to permit the marriage because Gibran had no money. Later in life, through letter-writing, he fell in love with another woman, but he was still too poor to go to Lebanon to be with her. This was also a time in his life when his health was poor. Gibran died in 1931. His books earned more than two million dollars, but much of this income came after his death.

Garments

Upon a day Beauty and Ugliness met on the shore of a sea. And they said to one another, "Let us bath in the sea."

Then they disrobed and swam in the waters. And after a while Ugliness came back to shore and garmented himself with the garments of Beauty and walked his way.

And Beauty too came out of the sea, and found not her raiment, and she was too shy to be naked, therefore she dressed herself with the raiment of Ugliness. And Beauty walked her way.

And to this very day men and women mistake the one for the other.

Yet some there are who have beheld the face of Beauty, and they know her notwithstanding her garments. And some there be who know the face of Ugliness, and the cloth conceals him not from their eye.[1]

[1]Kahlil Gibran, *The Wanderer His Parables and His Sayings* (New York: Alfred-A-Knopf, 1971) 5.

Student Activity
International Biographies
Book 1
Lesson 2, Handout 5
Sample

Name______________________

Date ______________________

Kahlil Gibran

On this page are some of Gibran's wise sayings. Read them carefully and try to understand what he is telling us.

Self-Knowledge: *Know your own true worth, and you shall not perish. Reason is your light and your beacon of Truth . . .*[2]

Advice: *He who does not seek advice is a fool. His folly blinds him to Truth and makes him evil, stubborn, and a danger to his fellow man.* [3]

Age: *Seek ye counsel of the aged, for their eyes have looked on the faces of the years and their ears have hearkened to the voices of Life. Even if their counsel is displeasing to you, pay heed to them.*[4]

Beauty: *Beauty is that which attracts your soul, and that which loves to give and not to receive . . .* [5]

Bravery: *Bravery is a volcano; the seed of wavering does not grow on its crater.*[6]

Learning: *Learning is the only wealth tyrants cannot despoil. Only death can dim the lamp of knowledge that is within you. The true wealth of a nation lies not in its gold or silver but in its learning, wisdom, and in the uprightness of its sons.*[7]

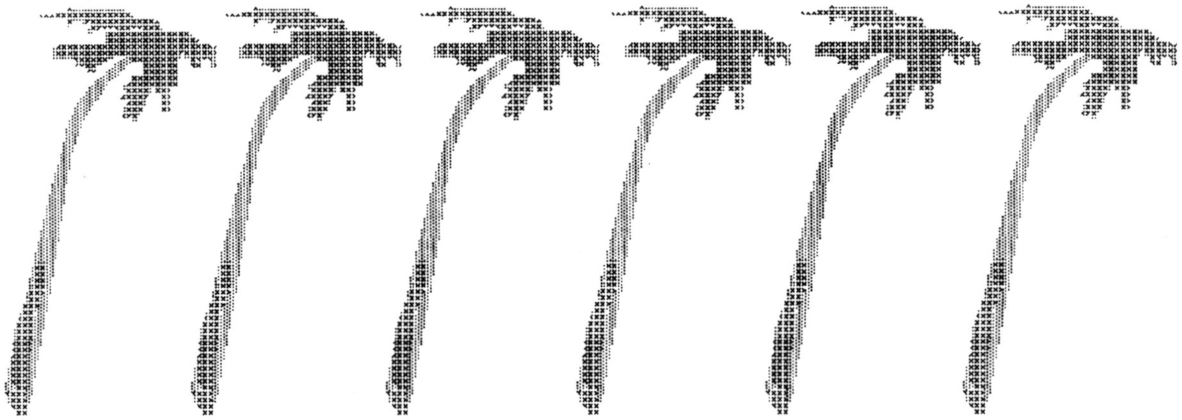

[2]Joseph Sheban, ed. *The Wisdom of Gibran: Aphorisms and Maxims* (New York: Philosophical Library, 1966), S–2.
[3]Ibid., A–1.
[4]Ibid., A–2.
[5]Ibid., B–1.
[6]Ibid., B–3.
[7]Ibid., L–2.

Student Activity
International Biographies
Book 1
Lesson 2, Handout 6

Name____________________

Date ____________________

My Philosophy Cube

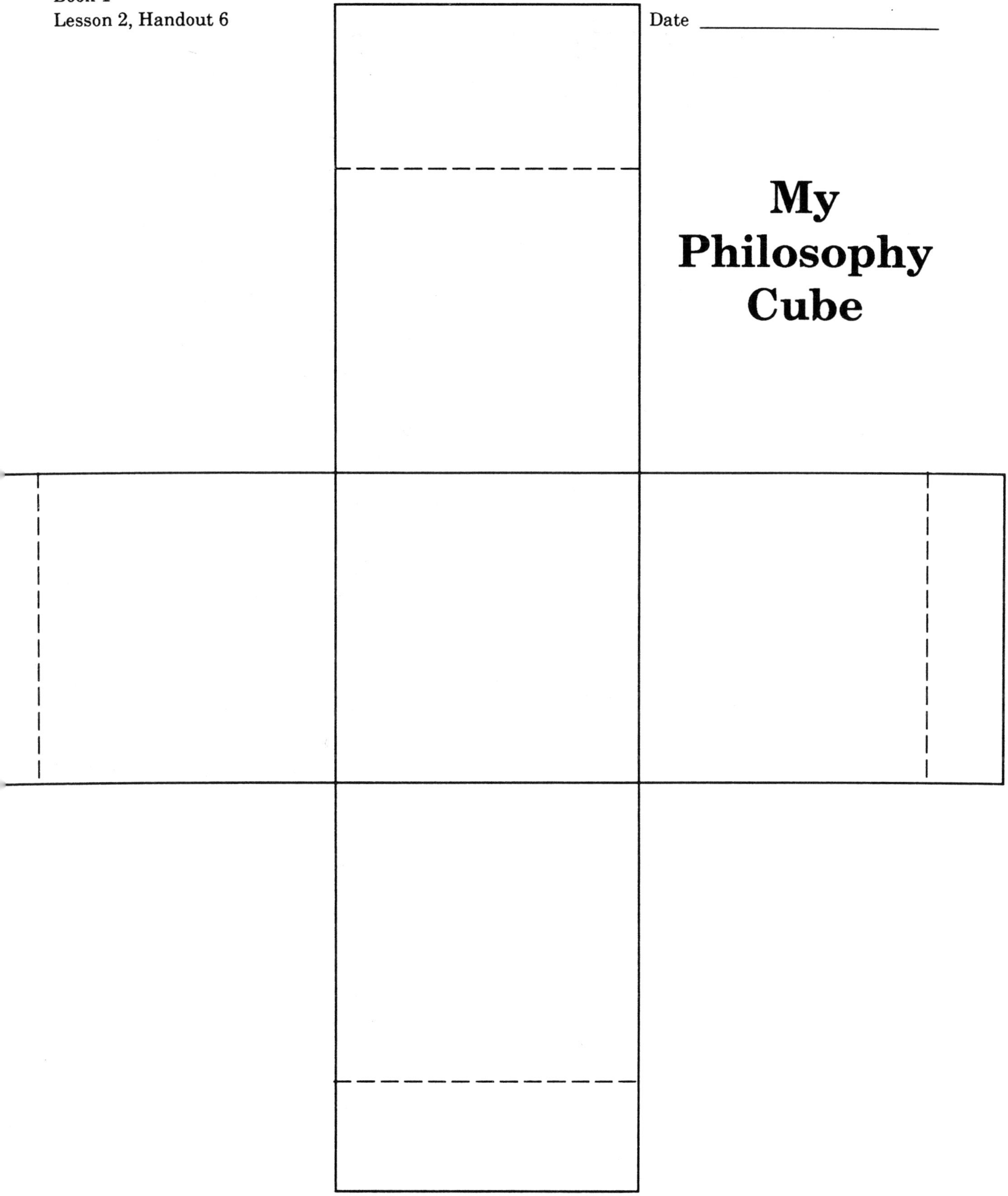

Jomo Kenyatta

Objectives

- To identify Jomo Kenyatta as a leader in Kenya's fight for independence
- To recognize the importance of symbols and to create personal symbols

Notes to the Teacher

It is helpful for students to have some understanding of the European colonization of Africa. They should know that Africa was carved into countries by Europeans without regard to different tribal units living there. This practice caused enemy tribes to be placed within the same boundaries competing against one another for their survival.

The white minority ruled these African colonies for the benefit of the white settlers who were encouraged to come there to farm, to mine and to trade. As a result there was much unrest. In the 1960s most African countries finally gained independence, but it was not won without struggle and strong men and women who were willing to fight to get it. Kenyatta was such a man—a villain in some people's view but a hero to his countrymen. He was the man who brought Kenya from its agrarian past into the modern age. After learning something of the man from his biography, the class might like to find out who saw him as a villain or as a hero and why. This could produce some provocative discussions.

In the activities the culture of Kenya is explored by playing an old African counting game and by examining a symbolic hat and belt often worn by Kenyatta. Students then design their own personal symbols.

INTERDISCIPLINARY STRANDS:
Art, English/Language Arts, Geography, History

MATERIALS:
Handouts 7, **8**, **9** and **10**, crayons or markers, egg cartons and dried beans (or other markers), small margarine containers, world wall map

TERMS:
anthropology, economy, famine, governess, gruel, independence, majority, midwife, minority, mission, parasite, status

Resources

Archer, Jules. *African Firebrand: Kenyatta of Kenya.* New York: Julian Messner, 1969.
Cox, Richard. *Kenyatta's Country.* New York: Frederick A Praeger Pub., 1965.
Friedman, Julian. *Jomo Kenyatta.*London: Wayland Publishers, 1975.
Murray-Brown, Jeremy. *Kenyatta.* New York: E.P. Dutton & Co., Inc. 1973.
Wepman, Dennis. *Jomo Kenyatta.* New York: Chelsea House Publishers, 1985.

Procedure

1. Play the Ayo game. Divide students into pairs and distribute an egg carton, forty-eight beans, and two small margarine containers for home cups to each pair. Use **Handout 7** to explain the directions.

2. Discuss the fact that the Ayo is a very old African game that spread into Middle Eastern and South American countries. This game was probably played by the man about which they will be reading.

3. Show pictures of Kenya including Mount Kenya, game preserves, and people from various tribes. Examine the climate and geography features. Using a world wall map, locate Kenya and if a physical map is available show the various physical features found in Kenya. As the discussion of the biography proceeds, locate the various places around the world where Kenyatta traveled (London, Nairobi, Europe, United States, Soviet Union).

4. Read **Handout 8** and discuss Kenyatta's story using the following topics:
   a. Imagine what life must have been like for Kenyatta. *(Once he was a goat herder and then all that changed as he became more educated and more aware of what his people needed.)*
   b. Determine if he believed his family was important. *(He loved his mother and brothers. He even brought his brother home to look after when his mother died.)*
   c. Compare the way the Kikuyu announced and celebrated the birth of a baby to the way families do it today.
   d. Refer to the movie, "Roots" and to Kunte Kinte's child and how he took her and held her up under the full moon and gave her a name.
      Why is a new baby a reason to celebrate?
   e. Why did some people dislike Kenyatta and want him jailed? *(He was trying to change things. People feared his power.)*

5. Examine **Handout 9** which shows the symbols Kenyatta wore to demonstrate his loyalty to the Kikuyu and the Luo Tribes. Talk about the use of symbols in a culture and why they are important.

6. Have students use **Handout 10** to create symbols to represent themselves and to write an explanation of the meaning of those symbols. (If they have a best friend, they might like to use fabric paints and make a tee shirt for their friend with their symbols on it. Then the tee shirts could be exchanged with their friends as a show of loyalty.)

7. Display symbols around the room.

Enrichment/Extension

1. Research the country of Kenya and/or Jomo Kenyatta. Create a picture album of the country featuring people and places. (See Appendix, **Handout 45** .)

2. Research Kenyatta's life and Martin Luther King's life and compare and contrast their approaches of getting equal rights for their people. Examine the different cultures and governments and determine what kinds of problems each dealt with and how they solved them. *(Both wanted to gain their rights through peaceful means.)*

3. Explain that the Kikuyu did not keep a calendar as we do, but instead marked each year by a particular event. For instance, one year a particularly sweet flower was in abundance, so they named 1895 the year of the sweet smelling flowers, one year was that of the great locust plague, the name of a great battle with the Masai was given to another. Research a *decade* of history in the United States and try to rename each year by the most important or spectacular event that occurred that year. Almanacs from that time period and other reference materials with brief summaries of annual events like *Time* and *Life* magazines, would be useful. If students work on different decades, they could be illustrated and used as a timeline on bulletin boards. They could also do oral presentations explaining why they chose the names for each of the years in their assigned decade. (This idea could be expanded to include world history.)

4. Other potential lessons relating to Kenya can be found in: "Kenya's Picture Safari," *World History and Geography, Book 1: The East* (Villa Maria, Pa.: The Center for Learning, 1990) and "New Imperialism: Race for Colonies in Africa," *World History, Book 3: 1815–1919* (Villa Maria, Pa.: The Center for Learning, 1986).

Art Notation

Jomo Kenyatta's portrait depicts him wearing a traditional African hat. Perhaps the small circle reflects the many small tribes which he welded into a unified nation represented by the large circle. (See Appendix, **Handout 58**.)

Name________________________

Date ________________________

Playing the Ayo Game

This is an old African game. It was played in most African countries and even spread into Middle Eastern and South American countries. It is usually played with a wooden board with twelve holes, two cups, and seeds. Since most of Africa is farming country, one can see why they played with seeds and when the seeds are placed in the holes, they say they are "planting" them.

Game Materials: An egg carton (the bottom half), two small containers (like margarine containers), and forty-eight seeds (beans) for each pair of players.

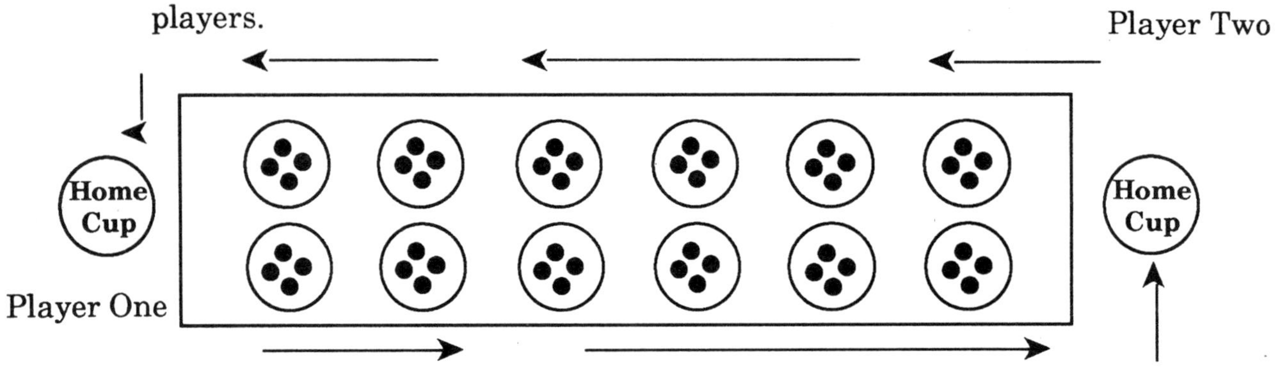

Set up: Each player is assigned one row of cups on the egg carton. Four seeds are placed in each cup. Play moves in a counterclockwise direction.

Begin: Player one picks up the seeds from any cup in his row and plants one seed in each of the next four cups moving in a counterclockwise direction. Player two does the same.

The game continues with each player moving all the seeds from any cup in his own row, and planting one seed in each of the next cups.

Object of the game: To capture as many seeds as possible from the opponents cups. To capture seeds this is what you do—

When your last seed is planted in your opponent's cup and you already have one or two seeds there—no more—then you may capture the seeds.

After you take these seeds, you may move backward and take the seeds from all the consecutive cups that have only two or three seeds.

Put the captured seeds in your Home Cup (small margarine tub). You win when you have twenty-four seeds in your cup.

Name________________________

Date ________________________

Jomo Kenyatta

Ten-year-old Kamau wa Ngengi was very ill. The medicine men in the little African village and even his grandfather, Kongo, who was a great magician with many powers, could not make him better. They had chanted and sacrificed animals and made him medicines from herbs, but nothing worked. What could they do now?

Name______________________

Date ______________________

Kamau, like all Kikuyu boys, ran barefoot and had picked up a parasite called jiggers. Then he developed an infection of the spine which weakened his whole body. He was going to die. His parents took him to the Scottish mission and the white doctors treated him. Soon he was well. He had learned many things while he was there. He was particularly interested in the reading and writing he saw the missionaries do. He wanted to learn more. Who was to know then that someday this little native boy would be known as Jomo Kenyatta, the first president of the independent country of Kenya?

Jomo was born near the end of the 1800s, but no one knows the exact date because the Kikuyu tribe did not record births and deaths. They marked their calendar with events that affected the whole community such as a famine or being overrun by locusts. Although the date was not recorded, the place of birth was important because the Kikuyu were farmers and herders and felt close ties to the land. Kenyatta was born twenty-five miles northeast of Fort Smith at Ngenda. His father was Muigai and his mother was Wambui.

When a Kikuyu child is born, a midwife washes and oils him and spits a mouthful of gruel into his mouth—to bless his life on earth. The mother screams five times to let everyone know that a son is born. The father hears the screams and cuts five sugar canes. A sheep is killed and a feast is held. The women brew beer for the occasion. Some is spilt on the ground for the spirits.

Jomo learned about the Kikuyu tribe from the stories and songs told to him by his mother at night in their mud hut. She taught him about the plants and animals that lived around them. From his father he learned how to take care of the fields and the sheep and goats that his family herded, to light fires, to plant crops, to gather honey, and to tell which trees gave the poison needed to put on the hunting arrows and which were good for building huts.

When Jomo's father died, his mother, as was the custom, married his father's brother. They had a child, but his mother took the child and went away to live with her family leaving Jomo and his brother with their uncle. When his mother who Jomo loved very much became ill and died, he rushed to her family and took his baby brother back home with him.

Name______________________

Date ______________________

At age twelve he went to live at the mission school. He knew that his world was changing and that he needed to read and write. He also became a Christian and took the Christian name of Johnstone. His Kikuyu friends still called him Kamau. A handsome young man with some skills, he went to Nairobi, a big town, to get a job. He liked the bright lights and the chance to make some money. He also knew that he could get more education in Nairobi. He married Grace Wahu, and they had a son. His job was reading water meters.

Kamau (Jomo) became involved with an African political group that wanted the Kikuyu lands that had been taken away and given to white settlers to be returned. They also wanted all laws to be printed in the Kikuyu language, taxes to be reduced and wages increased, and Africans to be allowed to raise coffee like the white settlers. Jomo was sent to London in 1929, to try to get the British government to make the settlers government in Africa listen to their demands. In London, Jomo got more education and met many important people who were interested in helping Africans.

Jomo was sent to London again in May, 1931. Since he had not been invited to speak to the committee discussing African affairs, he could not get into the meeting. He did go to several other meetings to speak about conditions in Africa and the problems with the colonial governments. He told them that most African countries were governed by European countries and the majority of blacks were being governed by a minority of whites.

No one seemed to care what the Africans thought of the laws or that their land was given to white settlers. Jomo Kenyatta was a man who did not want to use violence to get freedom. He believed that through reasonable discussion an agreement could be reached. He even got a degree in anthropology from the University of London so that he could show the white government that blacks were their equals and could handle their own affairs. He also wrote a book called *Facing Mount Kenya.* It explained much about tribal life and tribal beliefs.

He returned to Kenya after fifteen years and quickly became a leader of the Kikuyus. He also married a third wife, an English woman named Edna Clarke, a governess. His first two wives were Africans. The Kikuyu often had more than one wife if they could afford it—more wives meant more help on the farm. Edna understood and accepted this.

Name________________________

Kenyatta tried to keep his people from fighting but could not stop them. One group called the Mau Mau wanted to frighten the settlers and they were banned by the government. Many acts of terrorism were committed by the Mau Mau. Kenyatta was arrested in 1952, for being a part of the Mau Mau. They expected a fight, but Kenyatta was standing there with his hands stretched out for the handcuffs. He asked them why they had taken so long! (He had known they were coming but chose not to run.) He stood trial and some of the witnesses against him were paid to lie. He was found guilty and sent to jail.

His old friends continued to work for independence and the British began to allow the Africans to participate in the government. His friends insisted that Kenyatta be released. Finally in 1961 he was freed.

Kenyatta wanted all the tribes to work together to get independence for Kenya, and for awhile they did. He was elected prime minister and on December 12, 1963, Kenya won its independence from Britain. After they got their independence the tribes began to argue about how to take care of their problems. Because of the arguing, Kenyatta took more control of government operations. Some called him a dictator, but he feared the loss of independence if the tribes all fought among themselves. There was much poverty and although the young people now were getting some education, there were no jobs available. He needed the tribes to work together. The Kikuyu became the most powerful tribe, however, and angered the other tribes.

Kenyatta became an international statesman and a leader of Kenya. He tried to be friendly with both the United States and the Soviet Union. He both allowed the newspapers to print the truth, provided better schools and health care, some land was given back to Africans, people had more personal freedom, foreign investors began to bring money into Kenya, and the economy improved. When Kenyatta died on August 22, 1978, his people mourned him. He had led them into the modern age and in their fight for independence.

Student Activity
International Biographies
Book 1
Lesson 3, Handout 9
Sample

Name________________________

Date ________________________

Symbols of Jomo Kenyatta

When Jomo Kenyatta became president he wanted to unite the various tribes within Kenya. One way he made his point was to wear symbols representing two of the major tribes—the Kikuyu and the Luo. He always wore a Luo chief's hat that the tribe had given him and a beaded "kenyatta" around his waist as the Kikuyu wore. He, himself, was actually a symbol around the world for other countries—a symbol of the new independent Africa.

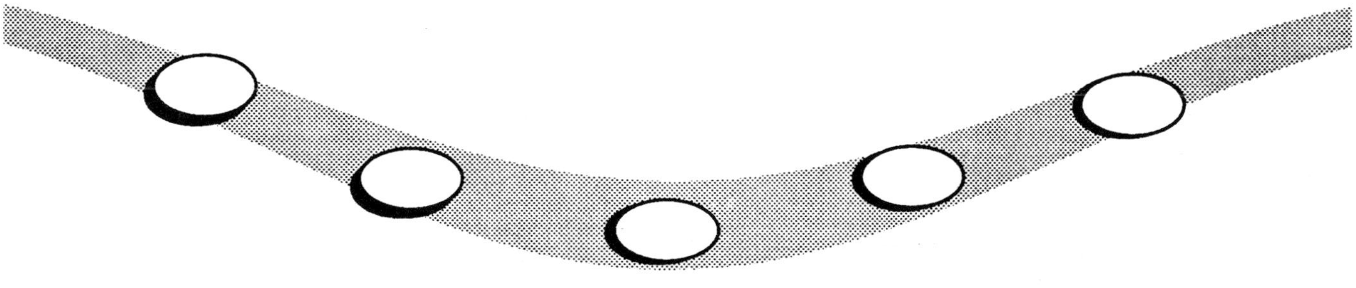

Name________________________

Date ________________________

Symbols of Who I Am

Lawrence of Arabia

Objectives

- To identify the role of T. E. Lawrence in gaining Arab independence
- To examine a crest designed for Lawrence of Arabia
- To design a family crest

Notes to the Teacher

In this lesson students read and discuss the role of T.E. (Thomas Edward) Lawrence who was instrumental in the Arabs becoming independent from the Turks after World War I. A brief overview of Britain's and France's role in the Middle East and Turkey's alignment with Germany during World War I is needed to put the Arab's fight for independence in perspective.

Although historians disagree on the importance of Lawrence's role and there is some suspicion about his motives, his romantic exploits gained him worldwide fame. His role at the peace conference of 1919 and in later conferences was instrumental in gaining Iraq for the Arabs. His acceptance and respect of Arab culture is an important point of emphasis, especially in relationship to the current conflicts in the Middle East.

After reading Lawrence's biography and discussing his life, students examine a crest that depicts his ideas, characteristics, and beliefs. They then design a crest symbolizing their family's characteristics.

INTERDISCIPLINARY STRANDS:
Art, English/Language Arts, Geography, History

MATERIALS:
Handouts 11, 12, and 13, marker and pen, world wall map

TERMS:
Arab, artifacts, crusades, Emer, motive, RAF, thesis

Resources

Graves, Richard. *Lawrence of Arabia*. New York: Charles Scribner's Sons, 1976.

Knightley, Philip. *Lawrence of Arabia*. New York: Thomas Nelson, Inc., Publishers, 1977.

MacLean, Alistair. *Lawrence of Arabia*. New York: Random House, 1962.

Procedure

1. Ask students if they have ever looked at clouds and seen different shapes or objects. What types of pictures did they imagine?

2. Explain that often we visualize things we have read about or dreamed about. Introduce Lawrence of Arabia as a British boy who dreamed of castles and the Crusades. Explain that the Crusades were wars which Christian from the West fought during the Middle

Ages to capture the Holy Land from the Arabs. It also means any fight for a cause thought to be good.

3. Locate the Middle East on a world wall map. Briefly discuss the geography of the area. Note the large areas of desert and the important oil fields. Locate the countries of Syria, Iraq, Jordon, Saudia Arabia, and Egypt. Explain that before World War I most of these countries were under the rule of the Turkish empire. Also locate Britain and Germany and explain that these countries were the two major combatants in World War I.

4. Read the biography of Lawrence of Arabia in **Handout 11**. Ask students to find out what crusade he fought and to keep in mind the background of World War I and the fact that he was British.

5. Discuss his biography using the following questions:
   a. What was Lawrence's crusade? *(independence for the Arabs)*
   b. Why did he feel betrayed by the British? *(The British had promised the Arabs the land they had fought for but gave them only a small part of Syria to rule.)*
   c. How did Lawrence's early life prepare him to lead the Arabs? *(He knew Oriental languages, studied the Middle East, was interested in military strategy, and knew and respected the Arab culture.)*

6. Inform students that during the Middle Ages many knights had crests that symbolized their beliefs and characteristics. Examine the crest designed for Lawrence of Arabia on **Handout 12**. Point out the symbols used for Lawrence: a castle—representing his interest in the Middle Ages; an Arab robe—representing his acceptance of Arab culture; and seven pillars—representing his book *The Seven Pillars of Wisdom.*

7. Have students use **Handout 13** to design their own family crest. Encourage them to use colors and symbols that represent their family's ideas, beliefs, talents, and interests.

8. Display the crests in the classroom.

Enrichment/Extension

1. View the movie *Lawrence of Arabia* and compare it to the text.

2. Pretend to be an Arab soldier under the leadership of Lawrence. Write a description of a typical day. Include the geography and culture of the Arab world.

3. Investigate current areas of conflict in the Middle East. Operation Desert Storm, the civil war in Lebanon, the Israeli/Arab conflict, Opec, and other current events can be found regularly in news articles. (See Appendix, **Handout 52**.)

Art Notation

Lawrence of Arabia's portrait depicts this Englishman in the traditional Arab garb which he wore much of his adult life. His energetic and forceful facial expression is reflective of his dynamic leadership. (See Appendix, **Handout 58.**)

Student Activity
International Biographies
Book 1
Lesson 4, Handout 11 (page 1)
Sample

Name________________________

Date ________________________

Lawrence of Arabia

The young boy lay on his back looking at the clouds overhead. One looked like a giant white castle with dragons and towers all around. He dreamed of knights in shining armor and great battles. He thought, "What an exciting time that must have been. If I lived during the Middle Ages I would go on a Crusade or I would lead an army and fight to bring glory and honor to the land of the Middle East." Little did the young boy realize that when he grew up, he would be doing just that—leading a fight to bring freedom to the Arabs of the Middle East. He would become the famous Lawrence of Arabia.

Name________________________

Date ________________________

T. E. Lawrence was born in Wales in 1888. His family moved often, but finally settled in Oxford, England. There, Ned, as he was called, went to school and to the university. As a boy he loved to read about the Crusades. He spent time traveling by bicycle through England to examine castles and he made brass rubbings of artifacts. He even became an expert in military strategy and shooting.

Lawrence attended Oxford University and specialized in oriental languages. To earn a degree about the military architecture of castles, he went to the Middle East to research castles. As he traveled alone and on foot, he was welcomed in many villages as a curiosity. Many Arabs had never seen an Englishman. After completing his research, he published his thesis under the title, *Crusader Castles.*

After graduating, Lawrence returned to the Middle East to work on archaeological digs along the Euphrates River. He grew fond of the Arab people and resented the domination of the Arabs by the Turks. In 1914 when World War I broke out, Lawrence joined the British army as a lieutenant in the Department of Intelligence. Due to his knowledge of the Middle East, he was sent to Egypt to draw maps. The British were fighting Germany and the Turks were on Germany's side. Lawrence was asked to talk to Arab leaders about staging a revolt against the Turks. Lawrence spoke Arabic and had adopted the dress and habits of the Arabs; therefore, he was accepted by them. He was successful in persuading the Arabs to revolt.

Lawrence discovered one man capable of uniting the many quarrelsome Arab tribes, Emar Feisal, a respected Arab and an able leader.

With Emir Feisal, Lawrence led a core group of about 600 Arabs on many raids. The group increased and decreased at different times, as different tribes joined for different battles. He was given gold by the British to distribute to the Arabs for their work, and he also permitted them to keep the loot from raids on the Turks. The Arabs fought by making sudden raids and then disappearing into the desert. Lawrence found this type of attack very effective in destroying railroad bridges and lines that were needed by the Turks. He himself was reported to have personally been responsible for destroying seventy-nine railroad bridges.
Very few Arabs were killed in these surprise attacks, but many Turks met their deaths.

Name____________________

Date ____________________

With brave leaders and faithful Arab tribesmen, Lawrence crisscrossed the deserts, raiding railway lines and villages. The Arabs sometimes went without sleep for several days, eating only a simple bread made from flour and water, and dates. They slept curled in the sand and often went for months before they could change their clothes. For some, the fight for independence was made easier by the payment of gold. But for Lawrence, the biggest motive was in taking important cities before the British arrived, for he had been promised that whatever land the Arabs took control of, the Arabs could have when World War I ended. As a result, Lawrence and Feisal led the Arabs in capturing Akaba and Damascus, as well as lesser cities, and organizing the government of the cities before the British arrived.

After Damascus was taken, Lawrence asked to return to England as his work was completed. After two years of strenuous desert warfare, the Arabs had regained control from the Turks. Lawrence did attend the 1919 Peace Conference in Paris as Feisal's adviser and interpreter. He was exceedingly disappointed that, despite Britain's promise, the Arabs were not given independence and Feisal was given only a part of Syria to rule, and that remained under French control. Even worse, in 1920 the French drove Feisal off the throne; but, in 1921, Winston Churchill, British statesman, asked Lawrence to go to Cairo with him to rectify the situation. Lawrence and Churchill arranged for the Arabs to be given Iraq, which is about twice the size of Syria. Feisal was elected king of Iraq, and his brother Abdullah became the ruler of Jordan. Lawrence's dream of an independent Arab nation was at last fulfilled.

Lawrence returned to England and began work on a book about the Arab revolt entitled *The Seven Pillars of Wisdom.* He was unhappy with his fame as Lawrence of Arabia and changed his name to John Ross and joined the Royal Air Force (RAF). When his identity was discovered, he joined the Tank Corps of the army as T.E. Shaw, but disliked it, and asked to be reassigned to the RAF. He eventually was accepted by the RAF, spent some time in India, and returned to England.

In 1935 after being discharged by the RAF, he was killed in a motorcycle accident. Travelling at a high rate of speed, he swerved and crashed to avoid two boys playing on a country road.

Although Lawrence never actually rode a white horse and wore armor in battle, he achieved his dream of being a crusader for freedom, and his courage and respect for the Arab people is well remembered.

Student Activity
International Biographies
Book 1
Lesson 4, Handout 12
Sample

Name________________________

Date ________________________

Lawrence of Arabia Crest

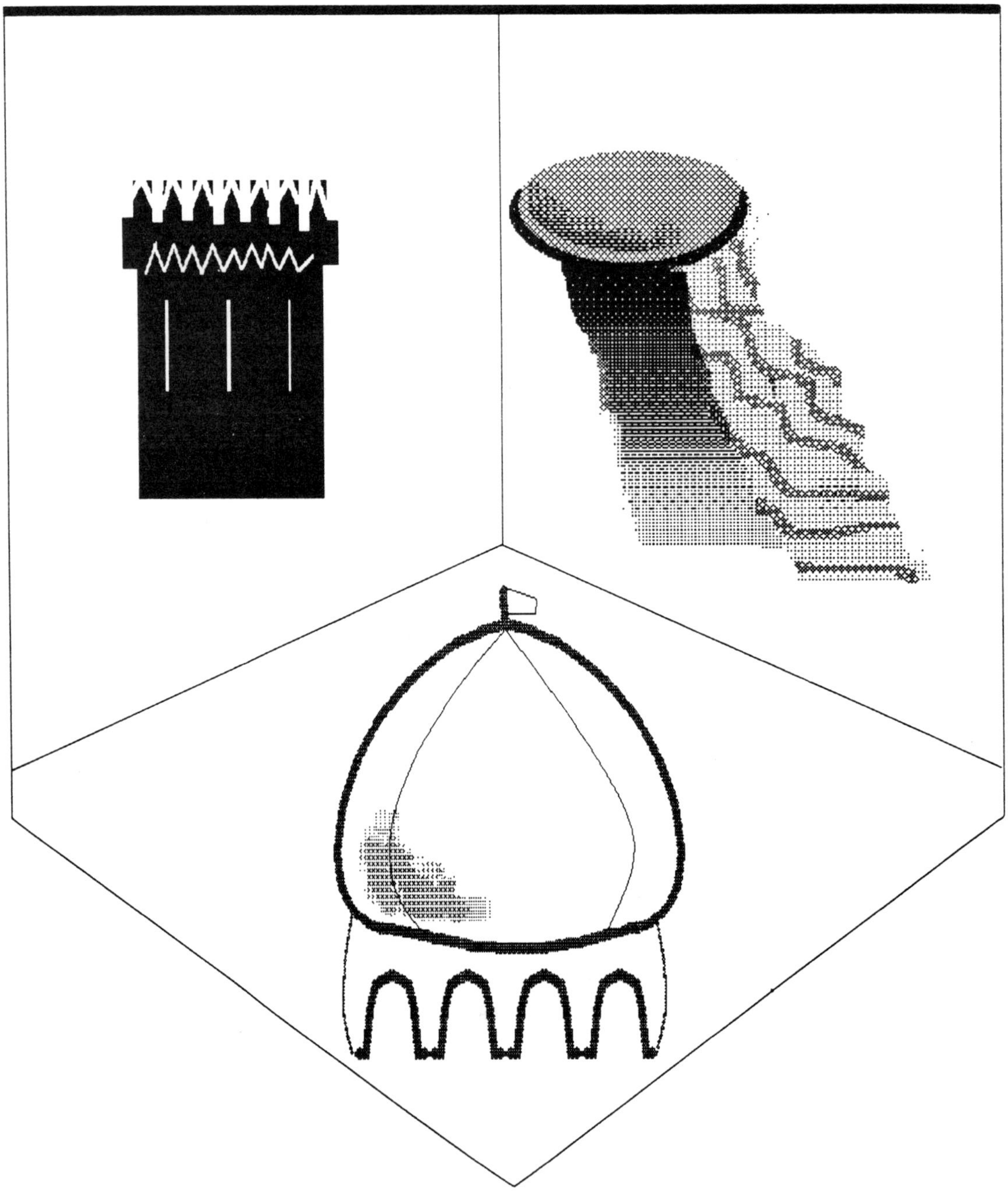

Student Activity
International Biographies
Book 1
Lesson 4, Handout 13

Name______________________

Date ______________________

My Family Crest

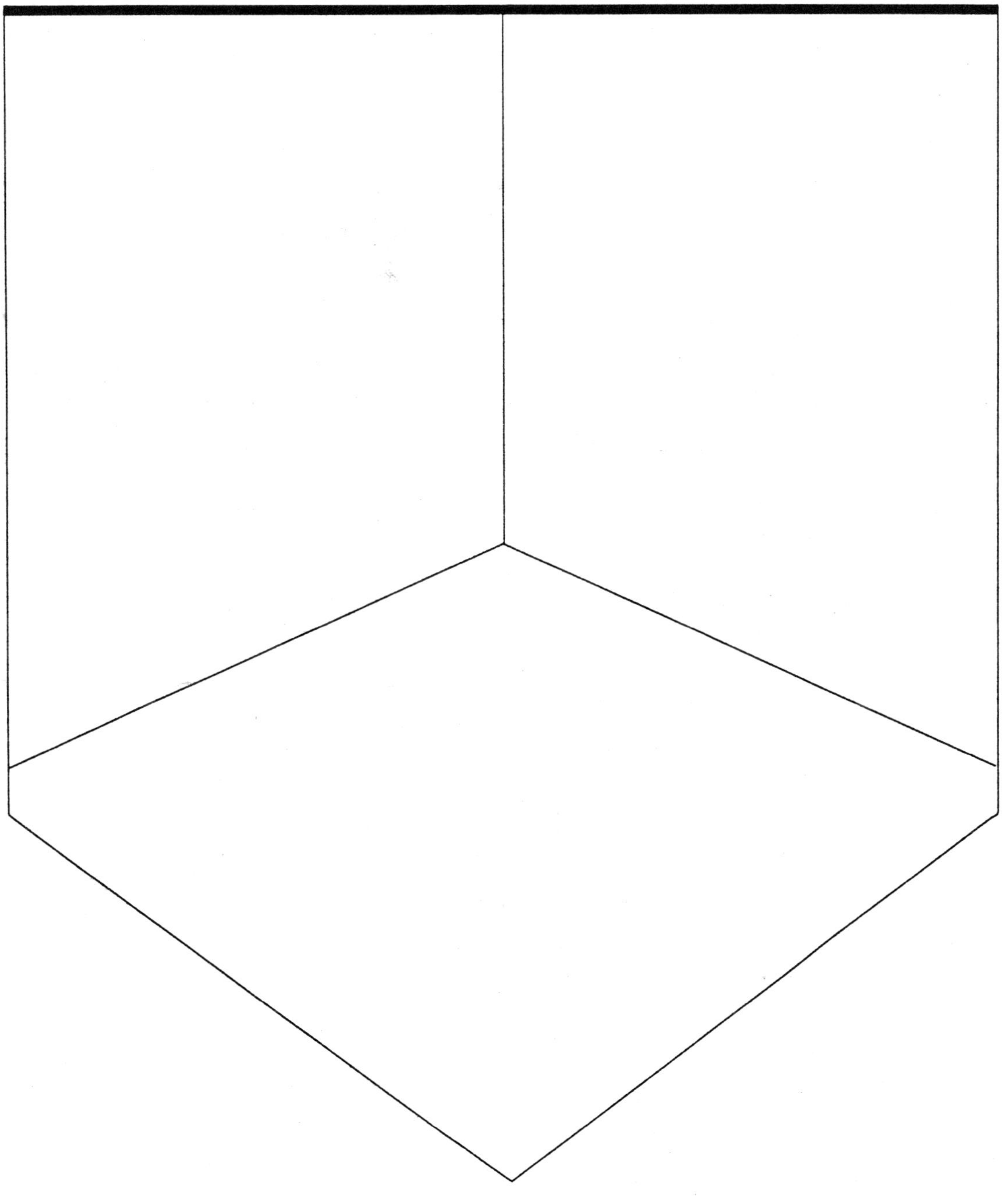

Miriam Makeba

Objectives

- To identify Miriam Makeba as a South African singer and political activist
- To recognize the influence an entertainer has on world opinion
- To create a necklace symbolizing your homeland

Notes to the Teacher

Miriam Makeba is known throughout the world as a singer and entertainer. Her outspoken support of the civil rights movement in the United States and the injustices of apartheid in South Africa have made her a controversial figure. Discuss the way Africa was colonized in the late 1800s by Europeans who saw the Africans as uncivilized and unable to think for themselves. Discuss the independence of African countries during the 1960s with the exception of South Africa and Namibia (freed in 1990). Also explore the system of apartheid in South Africa and the fact that it was almost a crime for a native to be successful there. South Africans did not want Makeba back in her country after she had achieved success because she was not the role model they wanted for their tribal peoples.

In this lesson students read a biography of Makeba and discuss how she used her fame as a singer to help the people of South Africa and the civil rights movement in the United States. They also discuss how things people wear reflect their culture and create jewelry that is symbolic of the United States.

INTERDISCIPLINARY STRANDS:
Art, English/Language Arts, Geography, History, Music

MATERIALS:
Handouts 14, 15 and 16, paper, glue, paint, crayons or markers, string, recordings of Miriam Makeba, world wall map

TERMS:
Afrikaners, apartheid, compound, consulate, culture, ghetto, passport, Swazi, thumbnail sketches, Transvaal, Xhosa

Resources

Canesso, Claudio. *South Africa.* New York: Chelsea House, 1989.
Jacobsen, Karen. *South Africa.* Chicago: Children's Press, 1989.
Makeba, Miriam with James Hall. *Makeba My Story.* New York and Scarborough, Ontario: New American Library, 1987.
Makeba, Miriam (selected by). *The World of African Song.* Chicago: Quadrangle Books, 1971.

Recordings

Miriam Makeba Sound Recordings, New York: RCA Victor, 1960. (sound disc, 35 min., 33 1/3 rpm)
Tangoam Sound Recording/Miriam Makeba, Burbank, California; Warner Bros., 1988. (sound disc, digital stereo or 33 1/3 rpm)

Procedure

1. Listen to a recording of Miriam Makeba or other African music. Discuss what the sound reminds students of and how the melody and beat make them feel. Introduce Miriam Makeba who used the culture and rhythm of South Africa in her music.

2. Use a large world wall map to locate South Africa. Ask students to share what they already know about the country. It is in newspapers frequently. Mention Nelson and Winnie Mandela and their fight against the apartheid system.

3. Read Makeba's biography in **Handout 14**. Locate the cities where Makeba lived: Johannesburg, Melspruit, Pretoria, and the Transvaal.

4. Discuss what students think has been the hardest thing Makeba had to face in her life *(loss of family, loss of country, divorce, death of loved ones).*

5. Divide student into cooperative groups. (See Appendix, **Handout 48.**) Have each group decide how Makeba's fame has helped her people in South Africa. Reconvene the class and ask a representative from each group to share their conclusions.

6. Ask students what they might do to draw attention to their own plight if they were to leave home and then be refused re-admission to their own country because of their fame as an entertainer. Remind students that Miriam Makeba's success made her an embarrassment and a threat to the authorities of South Africa. Discuss others who have been exiled by their homeland either officially (Alexander Solzhenitsyn) or unofficially (many people from Eastern Europe).

7. Inform students that Makeba often wore African clothes and jewelry that represented her homeland. Distribute **Handout 15** and talk about things that students wear that reflect their own culture. Note that subcultures also have traditional costumes. (motorcycle gangs, rock groups, square dance clubs, etc.).

8. Have students use **Handout 16** to design a necklace with symbols and pictures that represent their homeland..

9. Provide paper, string, and glue so students can create paper geometric shapes. Attach the shapes on string to create a necklace. Using their thumbnail sketches have students draw on their necklaces the designs they layed out in **Handout 16**.

10. Display the necklaces by having a fashion show during which students describe their necklaces and tell what each bead represents.

Enrichment/Extension

1. Research Nelson and Winnie Mandela and report how they have fought the apartheid system and how authorities have treated them. Reports can be written or oral. (See Appendix, **Handout 46.**)

2. Examine the United States' civil rights era in the 1960s and the legislation that resulted. Oral or written reports can utilize pictures taken during this time period. Also include current legislation that is related to civil rights.

3. Play selections from Paul Simon's *Graceland*. Discuss his role and the role of other entertainers in fighting apartheid.

4. Other potential lessons on South Africa and apartheid can be found in the following Center for Learning publications: "Apartheid", *World History, Book 4 1920–1985* (Villa Maria, Pa.: 1986); "Analyzing: Africa," *World Cultures / World History* (Villa Maria, Pa.: 1988); "A Case Study: Apartheid vs. Human Rights," *Current Issues in Global Education* (Villa Maria, Pa.:1988.)

Art Notation

Miriam Makeba's portrait depicts her as a world-acclaimed performer. The circle in the background represents the hot African sun. Although she is an international star, part of Miriam Makeba remains distinctly South African. (See Appendix, **Handout 58**.)

Name_______________________

Date _______________________

Miriam Makeba

Miriam Makeba was not happy. She was a famous singer known all over the world. She was rich. She had a lovely daughter. She performed before royalty. She sang at the White House. She was at the top of her profession. Why was she unhappy?

Name________________________

Date ________________________

She was unhappy because she was welcome in every country of the world *except* her own! It was not until 1990 that Miriam Makeba was finally allowed to return to her home in South Africa for the first time since she was a young girl. Today, she is one of the most influential women in Africa.

Her parents, Caswell and Christina Makeba, lived in Johannesburg, South Africa, and Miriam was born there on March 4, 1932. Her mother was from the Swazi tribe and her father was of the Xhosa tribe. Miriam was not expected to live, for her mother had been told to have no more children. She was weak, but cried loudly at her mother's slap that caused her to take her first breath.

Her mother, a nurse, named this sickly child Zenzi from the African word "uzenzile" which means "This is your own fault."[1] African children are named for something that is going on at the time of their births, and her grandmother kept saying "uzenzile" to Miriam's mom because she was warned to have no more children.

In South Africa, tribal and western cultures are mixed. Some people still live in small villages, but there are also large western style cities. Natives do not live in the modern western buildings, however. They live in ghettos nearby. They are paid poorly and the government keeps tribal people and whites separated in every way. Most laws are "racist"—against the African blacks or those of mixed descent called coloreds. This policy is known as apartheid.

When Miriam was eighteen days old her mother was arrested for making and selling homemade beer made from cornmeal. One of the apartheid laws in South Africa said natives could not drink because they were not 'civilized' enough.[2] Mrs. Makeba made beer to earn extra money. She had to pay a fine of eighteen pounds or go to jail for six months. She went to jail with Miriam in her arms.

They moved north to Melspruit in eastern Transvaal when Miriam and her mother got out of jail. Her parents worked in Melspruit. When she was five her father died suddenly. She, and three brothers and sisters, returned to her grandmother's compound in Pretoria to live. Her mother went to Johannesburg to work as a maid.

[1]Miriam Makeba, *Makeba My Story* (N.Y.: New American Library, 1987), 4.
[2]Ibid., 8.

Name______________________

Date ______________________

She grew up in the compound with twenty-one other grandchildren. They worked hard carrying water from the well, gardening, and cooking, and they ate mostly cornmeal dishes. There was a variety of fruit and greens. Rice was rare and served about once a week. They made rice custard and ate it with chicken on Sundays. They had no refrigerators so the rice custard was put under the floor on Saturday night to cool. Nights were cold in the Transvaal.

They were often disturbed in the night by police who searched for people living in the compound illegally without a "pass." This was part of apartheid. No one could travel without a permit, and if caught without one, a person was sent to jail. The police were Afrikaners, those of Dutch descent. They visited the compounds, day or night, to check for passes or illegal beer.

Miriam got to visit her mother in Johannesburg because she was young. Not everyone could go into the city because the authorities did not want too many natives there. If a man worked in the city, his wife could not visit him, but he could go home to see her if he got permission. If they saw each other illegally, the man was fired. This system was also part of apartheid. Miriam went in to town on a train just for natives.

Miriam loved music and sang in the church choir. At school, she hid in the back of the auditorium to listen to her sister sing in the school choir, but she could never be quiet. She would join in. She was put out many times until one day the choirmaster invited her to join the group.

When she was about twenty, Miriam began to sing with a group just for fun. She was alone now with a young daughter, Bongi. It was good to have something fun to do after work. Then she sang in clubs for pay and was offered a record contract in South Africa. She sang songs in several languages including her own Xhosa tribal language. In this language one of the sounds is a clicking sound made with the tongue. Many critics wrote about her unusual singing style.

She was invited to come to America to perform. It was a dream come true; she had seen American movies and she knew life was better there, but she had trouble getting a passport to leave because of the apartheid laws. Finally, she got approval, but she had to leave her mother and daughter in South Africa. She went to New York and was very successful. This really surprised this shy African girl. Makeba was also surprised when the South African government allowed Bongi to come to visit.

Name________________________

Date ________________________

Makeba sent her to a private school to catch up with her education. In South Africa, an apartheid law called the Bantu Education Act, had changed the educational system, and Bongi was not taught English and only a little reading and math. The government believed that uneducated tribal people were less trouble. Bongi caught up quickly in America.

Makeba became famous as a singer all over the world. Then her mother died. She went to the South African consulate to get her passport approved for the trip home. Her passport was marked invalid. She could not go home!

She continued her career in America and in other African countries. She also continued her fight for justice and an end to apartheid. She married Stokely Carmichael, a naturalized American. He was born in Trinidad, a British colony, and assisted the civil rights movement in the United States by doing benefits for Martin Luther King, Jr. She became an unofficial diplomat to the United Nations.

There were sad times as well—a divorce, the death of a young grandchild, and later, the death of her only child, Bongi. But Makeba continues to sing and continues to remind people of the kind of lives that are led by her people in South Africa. She is part of the movement which is bringing an end to apartheid there. She encourages other nations to speak out against apartheid. She doesn't lecture about her views, but the fact that she still sings and still remains free from South Africa's apartheid system makes her a symbol against racism.

Student Activity
International Biographies
Book 1
Lesson 5, Handout 15
Sample

Name____________________

Date ____________________

African-Style Jewelry

Makeba wore jewelry from her homeland. It could have looked like this. Use the next handout to draw symbols on a necklace that represents your homeland.

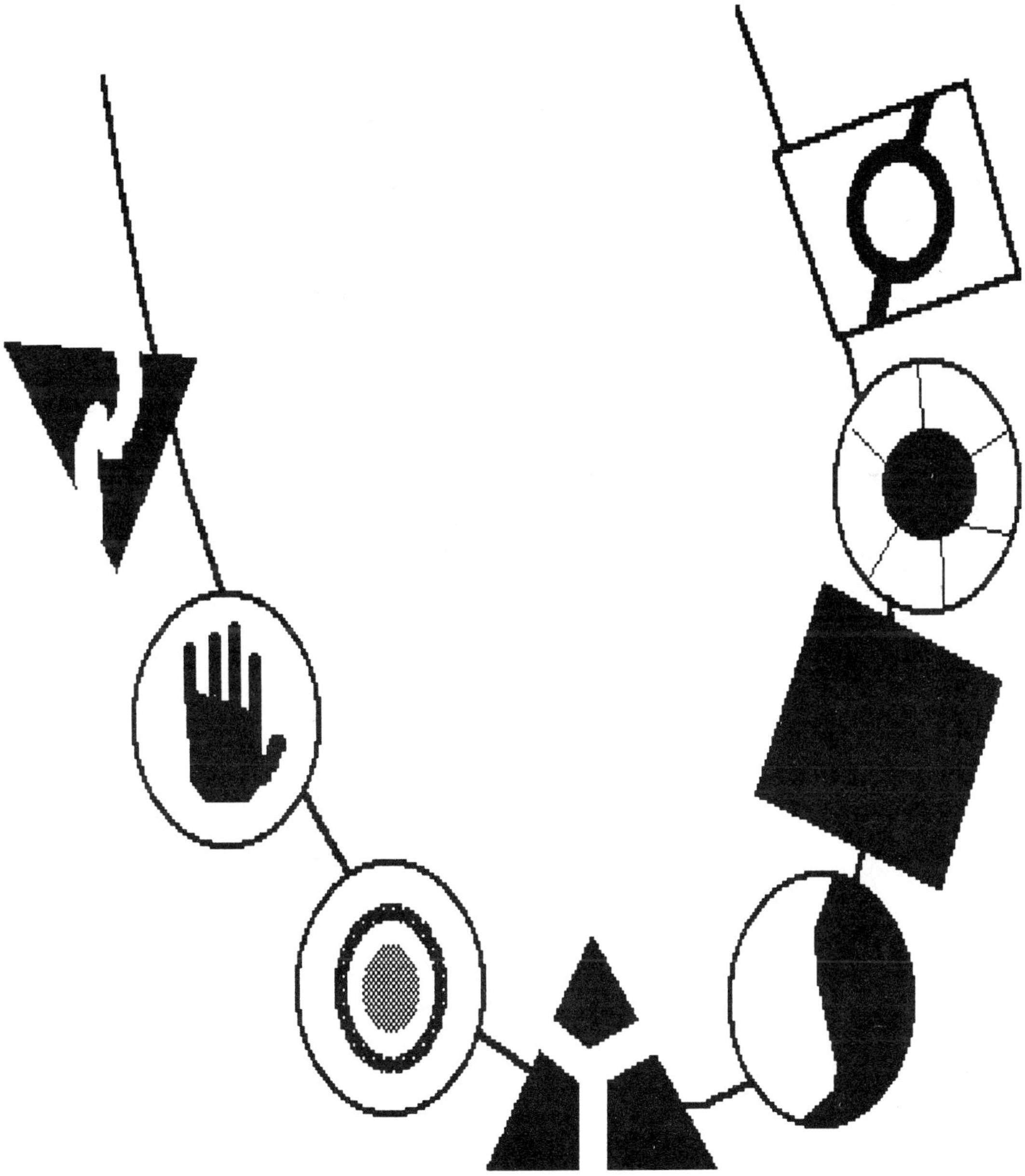

Name______________________

Date ______________________

Plan for My Country's Jewelry

Makeda: Queen of Sheba

Objectives

- To identify Makeda, the Queen of Sheba, as a ruler of ancient Arabia
- To discover the geography and trade routes of the empire of Sheba
- To chart a trade route between North American cities

Notes to the Teacher

There are many legends about the Queen of Sheba and who she really was. Most stories tend to name Makeda as the great queen who led the land of Sheba (also called SABA) and made an important trade agreement with King Solomon of Israel. The empire of Sheba was a large one, but Makeda wanted to extend its trade routes.

Sheba was located in southern Arabia in the area now called Yemen. Its capitol was Mariaba, also known as Mareb. Israel controlled important land and waterways that the queen needed. She, in return, possessed the rare incense that was burned in many religious ceremonies and was wanted by many countries. She traveled to Israel and met with Solomon who welcomed her. They discussed their individual countries and in an era of national aggression and domination made a peaceful agreement for trade. They also became friendly neighbors. Much of their story is written in the *Bible, Kings I, chapter 10.*

Students read about the life of Makeda, and are also introduced to the importance of negotiation. They review a map of trade routes and the empire of Sheba and then chart their own trade routes from their city to other trade centers.

INTERDISCIPLINARY STRANDS:
Economics, English/Language Arts, Geography, History

MATERIALS:
Handouts 17, 18, and **19**, globe, pencils, paper, world wall map.

TERMS:
agreement, amourous, archaeological, caravans, empire, frankincense, incense, myrrh, resins, retinue, talents

Resources

Pearn, Norman Stone and Vernon Barlow. *Quest for Sheba.* London: Nicholson and Watson Ltd., 1937.
Sertima, Ivan Van. *Black Women in Antiquity.* New Brunswick, USA: Journal of African Civilization, Transaction Books, 1984.
Silberman, Neil Asher. *Between Past and Present.* New York: Henry Holt & Co., 1989.

Procedure

1. The day before beginning the lesson, present the scenario below and assign the questions as homework. Imagine that tomorrow you are going to meet the wisest person in the world. You will have the opportunity to ask that person three, and *only* three, questions. What would you ask?

2. The following day, share the homework questions and have students tell how they decided what to ask the wisest person in the world. Introduce King Solomon as having a worldwide reputation, both then and now, as being a wise man. Inform students that they are going to read about a person who had the opportunity they imagined they had—she was able to meet and question the wise King Solomon. Point out that it involved a difficult journey for her.

3. Read the biography of Makeda, Queen of Sheba, in **Handout 17**.

4. Use a world wall map to locate the Arabian peninsula. Use **Handout 18** to locate the Queen of Sheba's empire. Note the countries of Egypt, Saudia Arabia, Yemen, Syria, Ethiopia, Armenia, and India.

5. Lead a discussion about trade and why it is important to countries. Discuss why it is important to seek a friendly relationship between neighboring countries and how this can be accomplished. Extend the discussion to Makeda and her trade agreement with King Solomon. What was the commodity traded by Sheba *(myrrh, frankincense, and incense)?* How did Sheba and Israel reach a trade agreement *(through peacefully negotiating and the trading of gifts)?*

6. Use **Handout 18** to locate areas along the trade route between Israel and Sheba. Note the geography of the Arabian peninsula *(mostly desert)* and discuss how goods could be transported between the two empires *(either by the Red and Mediterranean Seas and merchant ships or across the Arabian desert using camel caravans).*

7. Use **Handout 19** to locate the city the class lives in. Divide students into small groups (see Appendix, **Handout 48**) and ask each group to plan a trade route between their city and other major cities of the United States and Canada.

8. Have each group trace their trade route on **Handout 19**. Then ask a member of each group to show their trade route to the class on a large wall map of North America. Encourage them to explain why they chose that route and to point out cities and waterways along the route.

Enrichment/Extension

1. Research and discuss early explorers who traveled around the world in search of trade routes. (See Appendix, **Handout 45**.) Trace their routes on a large wall map.

2. Make a topographical map of the empire of Sheba. Indicate the desert regions and major waterways. Use appropriate symbols for countries of the areas such as a pyramid for Egypt, incense for Sheba, and a temple for Jerusalem. Display the maps.

3. Research the custom of burning incense at religious ceremonies. Bring in a sample and have the class experience its aroma and sensory features.

Art Notation

Makeda's portrait depicts her as a pretty young woman dressed in a turban and the attire worn in her area of Africa for centuries. History records that the queen presented King Soloman with many spices. The jar in the background represents the spice jars she might have used to transport her gift from Sheba to Jerusalem. (See Appendix, **Handout 58**.)

Student Activity
International Biographies
Book 1
Lesson 6, Handout 17 (page 1)
Sample

Name______________________

Date ______________________

Makeda, The Queen of Sheba

Jarod stood in the shade of the palace wall wiping the sweat from his face with the end of his sleeve. He watched as his wife Sarah came towards him. She was frowning and he knew why. Sarah had been busy all day packing the last of the queen's traveling clothes. She had been complaining for weeks about all of the things the queen "needed" to take—rich clothes for visiting King Solomon's palace, clothes to wear while riding the camel in her special traveling chair, night clothing, and on and on. Jarod smiled to himself as he remembered his wife's grumbling.

*The illustration of Makeda is based on a photo of a young Ethiopian woman.

Name______________________

Date ______________________

When Sarah reached his side, she began asking him about his part of the preparations for the trip. Now, it was his turn to complain!

"This journey will take us several months but we've packed so many things that you would think we are going to stay for years!" exclaimed Jarod. "I've built special containers to carry all the spices, precious stones, and gold. It has taken my men weeks of preparation, but we have finally finished. Everything had to be packed carefully so that nothing will be lost or damaged on the way."

Sarah nodded in understanding. "I had to make sure that the ladies-in-waiting packed Her Majesty's things carefully as well. She must look beautiful everywhere she goes—especially when she is presented at King Solomon's court and begins to question him."

"The camels are counted and those that needed to be trained have been trained. I finally found enough people for the caravan who can go to Israel with us," said Jarod.

"I hope all of these wonderful gifts satisfy King Solomon," sighed Sarah. "It would be a shame to waste so much time and energy on this trip, not to mention the rich gifts, and then fail to reach the trade agreement the queen wants. I hope nothing goes wrong."

Jarod laughed. He hugged Sarah and said, "Nothing will go wrong. We have checked and double checked everything. Tomorrow we'll be on our way at last."

Sarah looked at him and saw that he believed what he said. She relaxed and gave him a lovely smile. They went back to their final preparations for a trip that was destined to become a legend.

The queen who was the center of this legend was Makeda, Queen of Sheba, who ruled a large empire in the Middle East for over fifty years. Her empire included upper Egypt, Southern Arabia (where the capital was), Syria, Armenia, and eastward toward India. Trading was very important for her country. They traded by land, with caravans of camels carrying gold, jewels, and spices, and they traded by sea on large sailing ships called merchant ships.

During this time in history, incense was burned in many religious ceremonies. Incense was made from myrrh and frankincense, the

Name______________________

Date ______________________

aromatic resins of certain trees that only grew in Southern Arabia, where Makeda lived. The buying and selling of incense was the most important business the land of Sheba had. Makeda wanted to increase her country's trade. She had heard of King Solomon of Israel. Solomon was known as a wise and just leader with fabulous palaces. His kingdom of Israel was a powerful nation located on the Mediterranean Sea and on the northern end of the incense trade route.

Makeda wanted to meet Solomon, ask some questions of this wise man, and see the great country he led. She also knew that an agreement between their nations would strengthen trade. King Solomon controlled part of the Red Sea and the Mediterranean Sea. If she were allowed to safely travel on these, she could widen her trade and her country would be richer.

According to the legend, in 950 B.C., Makeda went to Jerusalem, the capital of Israel to meet with Solomon. Makeda carried with her large amounts of incense and 120 talents (about 4 million dollars today) to give to King Solomon as gifts. When Makeda arrived at King Solomon's palace, he treated her royally and according to the story, "entertained her honorably, lodging her and her retinue, seeing to it that she was fed generously and giving her eleven changes of garments daily."[1] It was reported that Makeda stayed many months at Solomon's court and many legends grew up around her stay.

One story tells that King Solomon was worried at first by rumors that his visitor, although beautiful of face, had feet that were like the hoofs of a goat. Anxious not to embarrass her, the king designed a plan to find out the truth: he ordered his worker to construct a crystal floor that looked exactly like water. When Makeda walked into the room, she instinctively lifted her skirts so as not to get them wet, and all could see that she did not have goat feet.

Another story is that the queen, being a virtuous woman, continually resisted the amorous advances of the king. One night, in desperation, Solomon fed her very highly seasoned food which made her very thirsty. He then placed a cool jug of water by his bed and an empty jug by hers. During the night, the queen, in order to quench her thirst, tiptoed into the king's room to borrow some of his water. She thus innocently placed herself within reach of the king who was awaiting her. The story contin-

[1]Lester Brooks, *Great Civilizations of Ancient Africa* (New York: Four Winds Press, 1971), 205.

Name________________________

Date ________________________

ues that after her visit to the King she did in fact become pregnant, and according to Ethiopian history, their son became Menelik I and was crowned first emperor of Ethiopia.

During her visit, Makeda talked with Solomon about religion, their countries, and trade. Solomon gave Makeda the rights to trade on the Red and Mediterranean Seas. Because of their trade agreement and friendship, the two countries also agreed to be at peace.

With new trade routes opened, the land of Sheba prospered. Makeda was a role model, not only as a woman leader, but also as a great negotiator. She knew what would strengthen her country's trade and worked with Solomon to accomplish this. Many leaders during her time of history were fighting to conquer and control land. Makeda knew that all nations needed each other to survive and remain at peace.

The legends surrounding Makeda may not all be true, but there is no reason to doubt that the Queen of Sheba was real. Some day archaeological research may confirm her existence and tell us more about this famous and wise queen.

Student Activity
International Biographies
Book 1
Lesson 6, Handout 18

Name________________________

Date ________________________

A Trade Route in Makeda's Empire

Use a globe or map to locate and label the following:

1. Red Sea, Mediterranean Sea
2. Israel, Jerusalem (capital of Israel)
3. Sheba, Mariaba(capital of Sheba)
4. Shade in yellow the Arabian desert.
5. Egypt, Saudi Arabia, Syria, Ethiopia, Armenia, India
6. Draw a trade route between the capital of Sheba and the capital of Israel.

Student Activity
International Biographies
Book 1
Lesson 6, Handout 19

Name________________________

Date ________________________

A Trade Route in the United States and Canada

Nelson Mandela

Objectives

- To identify Nelson Mandela as a leader in the fight against apartheid in South Africa
- To create a collage depicting key ideas and events in Mandela's life

Notes to the Teacher

Nelson Mandela is a South African lawyer and political activist who has come to symbolize the struggle for justice and freedom. In order to understand the struggle, students need to have some background on the European colonization of Africa and the system of apartheid. In the 1800s and early 1900s, European countries carved Africa into separate colonies and encouraged white settlement. The settlers took over the land and government of an area and the natives were left as second-class citizens with little or no say in how they were governed. After World War II, many African countries gained their independence, but in South Africa the minority white population still controls the government and the system of apartheid, while weakening remains. Apartheid is a system designed to keep the races separate. Whites have different housing areas, education, economic opportunities, and legal rights than blacks or colored (people of mixed race).

In this lesson students read about the life of Mandela and his methods of protest against the injustices of apartheid. After discussing the biography, students complete a timeline showing key events in Mandela's life. They also design a collage that illustrates his life. The collage is a visual representation that is enjoyable to construct and can also serve as a means of evaluating student knowledge.

INTERDISCIPLINARY STRANDS:
Art, English/Language Arts, Geography, History

MATERIALS:
Handouts 20, 21, and **22,** newspapers and news magazines, scissors, glue, paper, world wall map

TERMS:
African Nation Congress, Afrikaner, apartheid, banned, oppression, sabotage, sanctions, surveillance

Resources

Fortheringham, Allan. "The Lesson of Nelson Mandela," *McLeans* (Feb., 26, 1990): 56.
Hargrove, Jim. *Nelson Mandela: South Africa's Silent Voice of Protest.* Chicago: Children's Press, 1989.
Hewitt, Bill, and Hack, Susan. "Nelson Mandela," *People Weekly* (Feb. 26, 1990): 77–79.
Matthews, Tom, and Reiss, Spencer. "The Leader No One Knows," *Newsweek* (Feb. 19, 1990): 44–50.

Procedure

1. Ask students if it is legal in the United States to not give a person a certain job, live in a certain place, or go to certain schools because of one's race. Discuss why such practices are illegal and would be unjust. Then inform students that there are some countries in which racial discrimination is legal.

2. Locate South Africa on a world wall map. Briefly explain the European Colonization of Africa. (See "Notes to the Teacher.") Point out that South Africa was first colonized by the Dutch (Afrikaners) and later by the British. Also locate Johannesburg.

3. Ask students if they have heard of Nelson or Winnie Mandela. Discuss any information students already have on Mandela and then introduce him as a leader in the fight against injustice and oppression in South Africa

4. Distribute and read **Handout 20**. Discuss Mandela's method of nonviolent protest and his change to violent protest.

5. Have students focus on the key events in Mandela's life by completing the timeline on **Handout 21**.
   Suggested Responses:
   1918—born
   1930—went to live wirth his uncle, the tribal chief
   1936—began protesting and attended college
   1957—Apartheid laws established
   1957–1961—member of ANC (worked to end apartheid)
   1962 —arrested and sentenced to life in prison
   1982 —permitted to see his family without barriers
   1990s —current events (student research)

6. Explain the collage technique of arranging pictures and words in a pleasing way in order to convey a message. Have students use **Handout 22** to focus on the pictures and words they need to illustrate Mandela's life. Ask students to check their lists while they search magazines and newspapers for appropriate pictures and words.

7. Invite students to show their collages. Encourage them to explain why they selected particular pictures and words. Display the collages.

Enrichment/Extension

1. Debate the merits of nonviolent vs. violent protest or whether or not the United States should participate in sanctions against South Africa. Encourage students to research the issues so that they have facts to support their positions.

2. Research and report on other black South African leaders (Bishop Desmond Tutu, Alan Bosik, Oliver Tambo, Walter Sisulie etc.). (See Appendix, **Handout 45**.)

3. Show the movie (or selected parts) *Cry Freedom* and use it as a springboard to discuss Steve Beho.

4. Have students make a timeline showing the important events in their lives. (See Appendix, **Handout 51**.)

5. Other potential lessons on South Africa and apartheid can be found in the following Center for Learning publications: "Apartheid," *World History, Book 4 1920-1985* (Villa Maria, Pa.: 1986); "Analyzing: Africa" *World Cultures / World History* (Villa Maria, Pa.: 1988); and "A Case Study: Apartheid vs. Human Rights," *Current Issues in Global Education* (Villa Maria, Pa.: 1988).

Art Notation

Nelson Mandela's portrait depicts him as a contemporary leader who is actively engaged as an agent for change. His clenched fist represents the fight he has led to break the circle of South Africas's apartheid. (See Appendix, **Handout 58**.)

Name________________________

Date ________________________

Nelson Mandela

On a warm day in February, 1990, Nelson Mandela stood in front of a South African prison. After almost thirty years in prison, he was finally free! Mandela's release was noted by millions of people. While in prison he had become a symbol of the fight against oppression and injustice not only in South Africa but throughout the world.

Name____________________

Date ____________________

Nelson Mandela was born into the royal family of the Thembu tribe in 1918 in South Africa. When his father died in 1930, Nelson was sent to live with his uncle, the tribal chief. Educated at missionary schools, he often listened to his uncle decide tribal conflicts and became interested in studying law.

When Nelson was a college student, he participated in protests against laws that limited the power and freedom of native peoples. He joined a strike protesting the limited power of his college's student council and was suspended. When Nelson returned to his uncle's house, his uncle wanted Nelson to return to school. Instead, Nelson moved to Johannesburg.

In Johannesburg, Nelson married a nurse named Evelyn Ntoko Mase. He called the African National Congress (ANC). This group was interested in changing South Africa's racist policies. Despite the group's efforts, more *discriminatory laws* were passed in 1948 and a system called apartheid was established.

Under apartheid the races are kept separate. Whites, or Afrikaners, have different housing, education, economic opportunities, and legal rights than the blacks, colored (those of mixed races), and Indians. Mandela and other members of the ANC campaigned against apartheid. Mandela and others were arrested. The government banned Mandela because of his activities. This meant he was restricted to the Johannesburg area, could not speak at meetings, and had to resign from the ANC. During this time, Mandela also had trouble at home. His wife wanted him to give up his political activities. Eventually they separated and divorced.

Despite his troubles Mandela continued to work against apartheid. He was charged with being a communist and his trial lasted for over four years. (In 1961 Nelson was found not guilty, but he was still subject to the banning order.) During the trial he married his second wife, Winifred Mandikzela, a social worker. Winnie joined the ANC Women's League and was imprisoned on different occasions for protesting.

After the trial the ANC held secret meetings in homes and businesses and stayed on their course of nonviolent protest. But in 1960 their tactics changed. During an event known as the Sharpeville Massacre, the police killed sixty-eight peaceful protestors. As a result, the ANC changed from nonviolence to acts of sabotage. Mandela became head of a new activist group called Unhonto we Sizwe (Spear of the Nation). Mandela was

Name________________________

Date ________________________

careful to make sure no people would be hurt, but he did arrange for the destruction of buildings, and organized protests, work stoppages, and other acts of sabotage.

Mandela could spend little time with Winnie and his children because the police had them under surveillance. In 1962, the police finally arrested Mandela, tried him, and sentenced him to life in prison.

The government thought that by imprisoning Mandela, he would be unable to carry on his anti-government activities. Little did they know the courage and determination of the man. Mandela became a symbol of the fight against injustice not only to black Africans, but to the world.

Many people continued to try to change the apartheid laws. Through the years, other countries took interest in the unjust policies of South Africa. Some, including the United States, issued sanctions against trading and investing money there.

Gradually, the South African government began to seek ways to release Mandela. They offered release if he would stop planning activities against the government, but Mandela refused. In 1982 his family was permitted to see him in person, with no glass barrier. It had been twenty-two years since they had been that close. Finally, in February of 1990, Nelson Mandela was released.

Shortly after his release, Mandela traveled to fourteen countries, including the United States. He encouraged others to continue their sanctions against South Africa, and he raised money so that he could return to South Africa to continue the battle against injustice and oppression. Negotiations with the government began to start the process of ending apartheid.

Name________________________

Date ________________________

Timeline of Nelson Mandela's Life

Date	Event
1930	born
1936	began protesting and attended college
1957–1961	apartheid laws established
1982	arrested and sentenced to life in prison
1990	

Name________________________

Date ________________________

My Plan for a Nelson Mandela Collage

I need pictures of

1. ____
2. ____
3. ____
4. ____
5. ____
6. ____

Important words/phrases are

1. ____
2. ____
3. ____
4. ____
5. ____
6. ____
7. ____

Mansa Musa

Objectives

- To identify Mansa Musa as an emperor of the ancient African kingdom of Mali
- To explore the importance of trade to the people of Mali
- To design a trade caravan

Notes to the Teacher

This lesson deals with an early emperor of one of Africa's ancient kingdoms. Mansa Musa was a strong and able leader who ruled his empire wisely and fairly. Be aware that some of the spellings for the different place names and people's names varies within the different texts used for research. For example, Timbuktu is also spelled Tombouktou. Depending on maps used and student maturity level, discussion of these variations may be necessary.

Geography and economics are important strands on this lesson along with the culture of the people in the kingdoms. Secure books about Mali that show the ancient kingdoms and others that show modern Mali. Discuss the climate and the natural resources and their importance to the people. Help students understand the economics strand—trade and the influence of the amount of money (gold) in circulation upon its value. In the activity students examine the salt trade of Mali and identify other items that could be used as trade.

INTERDISCIPLINARY STRANDS:
Art, Economics, English/Language Arts, Geography, History

MATERIALS:
Handouts 23, **24**, and **25**, white and gold construction paper, world wall map, pictures and books about Mali, crayons/markers

TERMS:
Allah, calabash, caravan, empire, hostages, Islam, Moslem, oral history, profits, sovereign, sultan, trade

Resources

Brooks, Lester. *Great Civilizations of Ancient Africa.* New York: Four Winds Press, 1971.

Cable, Mary and the editors of Tree Communications, Inc. *The African Kings.* Chicago Ill.: Stonehenge Press Inc., 1983.

Davidson, Basil and the editors of Time-Life Books. *African Kingdoms.* New York: Time Inc., 1966.

Dobler, Lavinia & Brown, William A. *Great Rulers of the African Past.* Garden City, N.Y.: Zenith Books, Doubleday & Co., Inc., 1965.

Maalouf, Amin. *Leo Africanus.* New York: W.W. Norton & Co. 1986.

O'Toole, Thomas. *Mali . . . in Pictures.* Minneapolis: Lerner Publications, Co. 1990.

Procedure

1. Create trade items, salt and gold, by cutting blocks of white and gold construction paper.

2. Divide the class into four groups (see Appendix, **Handout 48**) and distribute the salt to two groups and the gold to the others. (There should be twice as much gold as salt.)

3. Tell the groups with salt that they must trade it for the gold with the other groups, but they are not allowed to talk to each other. Tell them that each gold piece is worth about twenty dollars and that those with the gold need salt in their diet to survive. Those who have the salt need the gold to buy things that they need.

4. Allow groups to work at their trade for a few minutes. Then, discuss their methods of trade. Did they try to use sign language? What did they do to reach agreement without voices?

5. Have them trade a second time. Compare the two rounds of trade. Did they do better the second time? Why? Why not?

6. Explain that the exercise they just completed was similar to the way Arabs and Africans conducted their gold-for-salt trade in the ancient kingdom along the Niger River around 800 A.D. Historians refer to it as "The Silent Trade." The Arab traders came on their camels with loads of salt. They placed large slabs of salt weighing two or three hundred pounds on the shore by the river. Each trader marked his pile of salt. Then they pounded a drum and rode away. After the Arabs left, the Africans came in their boats and placed gold by the salt and then left. When the Arabs returned, they decided if enough gold was left. If there was not a satisfactory amount the Arabs left again and waited. The Africans placed more gold by the salt and rowed away. If the amount was correct, then the Arabs picked up their gold and left, and the Africans came back and loaded the salt into their boats. Everyone was satisfied with the price and not a word was spoken. Thus it is called "The Silent Trade."

7. Discuss why the Arabs and Africans may have used this method. *(They should consider the fact that these people came from different parts of Africa and probably could not speak the same languages.)*

8. Explain that great kingdoms developed and controlled trade routes. Distribute **Handout 23** and have the students read about Mansa Musa, a king of one of these ancient empires.

9. Trace Musa's route from Mali to Mecca on a large map or overhead. Locate and name the countries that occupy that area of West Africa today. Note the Niger River and the cities of Timbuktu, Gao, Cairo, and the Sahara desert. Discuss the kind of land over which he would have traveled and what kind of climate differences he would have encountered. How might these differences have affected Musa's trip? *(Kind of clothes they needed: kind of foods that would be available and the type of preservation necessary to keep that food; kind of transportation needed, etc.)*

10. Discuss the influence Musa's gifts had upon the city of Cairo. Explain that inflation occurs when too much money (gold) is allowed into the system. Then it is no longer a scarce item and is no longer as valuable because there is so much of it. Have students think about and discuss what effect too much currency would have in their own country.

11. Distribute **Handouts 24** and **25**. Have students examine the sample sheet and discuss the salt trade. Instruct them to complete **Handout 25** by drawing in items that would have been taken on a caravan in Mansa Musa's time. Or have them draw items that are produced in Mali today that could be taken to market by caravan. (The caravan could also be an imaginary one from the local area. Students could research their own area and load a caravan with items they could find nearby to take to market.)

12. Display the finished camels around the room in a single-file line to make it look like a caravan. A background scene can be added.

Enrichment/Extension

1. Research other methods of trading and determine what other items were used as a medium of exchange instead of gold and what method was used to trade. Explore that same idea with Native Americans, early settlers in the United States, or other countries.

2. Determine what items the United States trades with other countries of the world and what we get in exchange. Make a list of imports and exports.

3. Report on the way our money system of currency and coins developed. (See Appendix, **Handout 45**.)

4. Other potential lessons relating to the country of Mali can be found in: "Mali: The Medieval Kingdom of Africa," *World History, Book 1: Beginnings to A.D. 1200* (Villa Maria, Pa.: Center for Learning, 1986) and "North Africa: Crossroads of Africa," *World Cultures and Geography* (Villa Maria, Pa.: Center for Learning, 1988).

Art Notation

Mansa Musa's portrait depicts him as the powerful rich ruler of the kingdom af Mali. His pensive almost prayer-like demeanor reflects the piety that led to his famous pilgrimage to Mecca. The Spanish-style crown and scepter represent the influence of the outside world on West African society. (See Appendix, **Handout 58**.)

Name________________________

Date ________________________

Mansa Musa

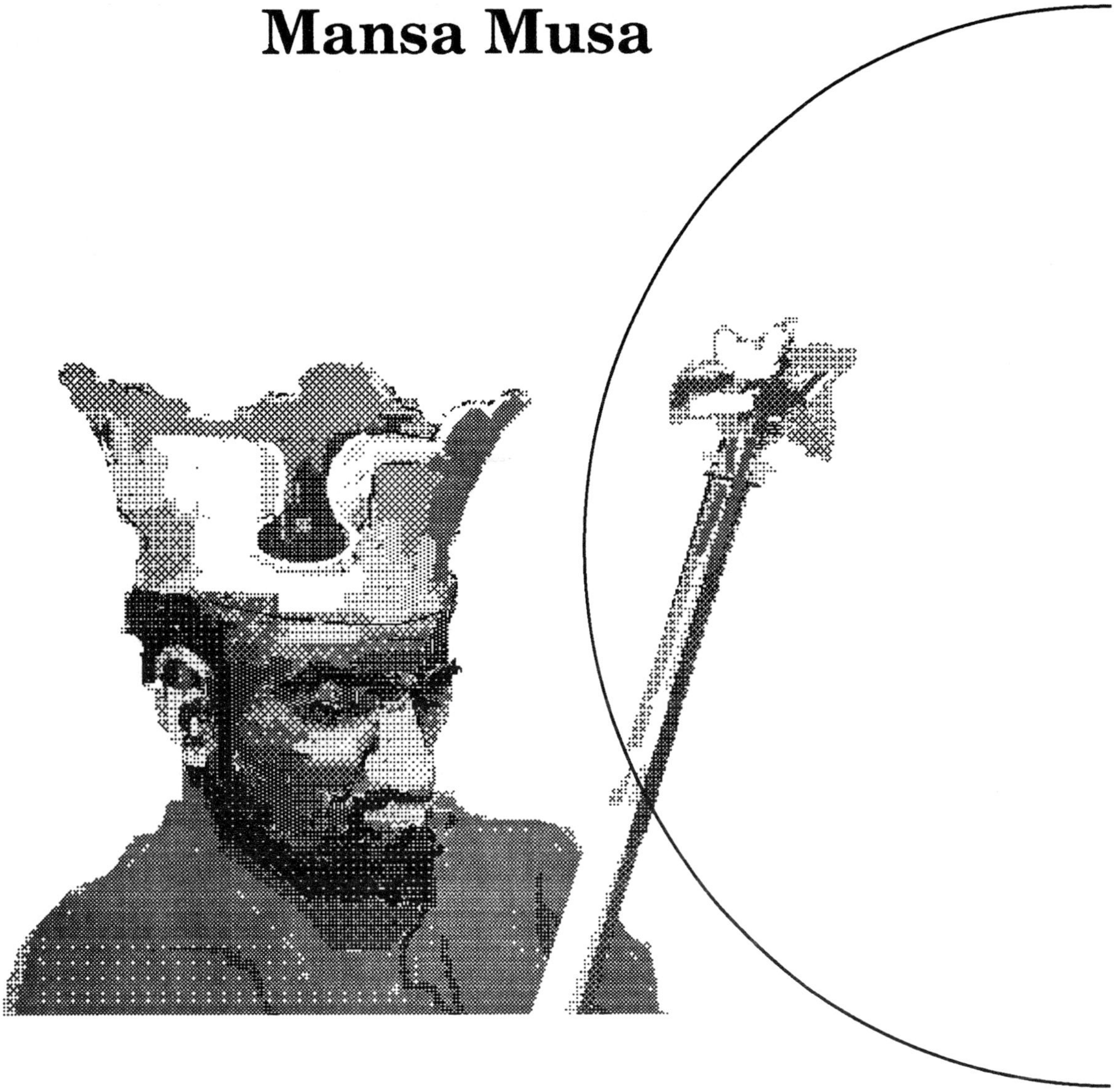

*

Have you ever heard of a faraway place called Timbuktu? Or a country called Mali? Or an emperor called Mansa Musa? All of them can be found on another continent and in another time. Mansa Musa was the ninth emperor of the ancient African kingdom of Mali located in the Western part of Africa, known as the Western Sudan. We do not know much about him before he became the emperor in 1312, except that he was a member of the Mandinke tribe. He was the grandnephew of Sudiata, and Musa came to power when his father Abu Bakr II died.

*The illustration of Mansa Musa is based on an artist's representation.

Name____________________

Date ____________________

His granduncle Sudiata was a little boy when Mali, was taken over by the country of Sossos. Sudiata's name meant "Hungering Lion," but he was a crippled child who could not even stand alone. The Sossos king spared his life because of his condition. Sudiata promised himself that one day he would get back his country and free the Mandinke people from the heavy taxes and the mistreatment they had under the rule of the Sossos.

Sudiata forced himself to exercise and to practice walking until finally he could walk alone. Then with the help of an army from a neighboring country, he began a five-year-fight to reclaim Mali for the Mandinke people. He was successful in defeating the well-equipped army of Sosso and moved the capital to Mali on the Niger River. Sudiata's sons and grandsons did not do a good job in ruling the country, and it looked as though their rule might end until Mansa Musa came to power. Mansa means emperor or sultan and Musa is an Arabic word meaning Moses. Like the Hebrew prophet, Moses, Mansa Musa was to save his people.

Mansa Musa, like all of the Mandinke people, was a Moslem. According to Egyptian historians, he was the most important black king in Africa. He held the largest territory and had the biggest army. He was rich and powerful and was feared by his enemies. He was able to help those who were close to him.

Mali's economy depended on the caravans that traveled from Mali to the lands in the north. They traded salt with the countries in the interior of Africa for gold. The gold made Mali very rich. The people of Mali also raised and sold crops of peanuts, rice, sorghum, taro, yams, beans, onions, calabash, and grains, as well as cotton, for a good profit.

Mansa Musa restored law and order to Mali. His armies extended Mali's borders west to the Atlantic Ocean, north to the Sahara Desert, and east to the cities of Timbuktu and Gao. They went south to take control of all the gold-producing areas. Within his kingdom, which was about the size of Western Europe, were about twenty-four smaller kingdoms left under the control of their own governors if they were loyal or under governors Mansa Musa appointed. His system worked. Peace was maintained and Musa established a fair tax system.

Mansa Musa's capital was at the crossroads of a trading system with the Arab countries of Morocco, Egypt, and North Africa. The Moslem world they found in Mali made these traders feel at home and welcome in the city.

Name____________________

Date ____________________

Al Omari, an Egyptian who saw Mansa Musa at his capital, described a day in his court:

> . . . Mansa Musa holds court in his palace on a great balcony called bembe where he has a great seat of ebony that is like a throne fit for a large and tall person. On either side it is flanked by elephant tusks turned towards each other. His arms stand near him, being all of gold, saber, lance, quiver, bow and arrows. He wears wide trousers made of about twenty pieces of material of a kind which he alone may wear. Behind him there stand about a score of Turkish or other pages bought for him in Cairo. One of them, at his left, holds a silk umbrella surmounted by a dome and a bird of gold: the bird has the figure of a falcon. His officers are seated in a circle about him, in two rows, one to the right and one to the left; beyond them sit the chief commanders of his calvary. In front of him there is a person who never leaves him, who is his official executioner; also another who serves as intermediary (spokesman) between sovereign and subjects, and who is named herald. In front of them again, there are drummers. Others dance before their sovereign, who enjoys this, and make him laugh. Two banners are spread behind him. Before him they keep two saddled and bridled horses in case he should wish to ride . . .[1]

Mansa Musa was also a very religious man, and like all religious Moslems, wished to go to Mecca, the holy city of Islam. Friends, family, doctors, princes, and tribal chiefs accompanied Musa on his great journey of about nine thousand miles. Some historians say that from eight to sixty thousand people went on this journey.

The journey required great preparations. The travellers had to gather food and supplies and prepare the caravan. They took gold dust from the royal treasury and divided it into sacks to load on the camels. Each camel would carry 300 pounds of gold. Musa's 500 slaves each carried a staff of gold that weighed about five grams. It took months to prepare for this journey that would take about a year to complete.

When the caravan reached Cairo, Musa was invited to visit the sultan. He did not wish to do so but finally consented after some discussion with the sultan's representative. When he arrived in the sultan's presence, however, he refused to bow down and kiss the ground before him. Finally, a wise man came up and whispered something to Musa and he consented to bow down by saying that he was bowing to Allah, not to the sultan.

[1]Lester Brooks, *Great Civilizations of Ancient Africa* (New York: Four Winds Press, 1971), 132.

Name_______________________

Date _______________________

(Musa did not wish to bow before the sultan because Cairo was not as important as Mali and the entire country of Egypt was not as large or as rich as Musa's empire. He felt he was an important African emperor who should not have to bow before an unimportant sultan.)

Before Musa left Cairo, the sultan sent him and his group many gifts of silver coins, camels for cargo, and camels for riding—complete with saddles and much food. In return, Musa saw to it that everyone in the sultan's court was given a gift of gold. Those in the city also received gold through the buying and selling of their goods to those on the caravan. Cairo had so much gold brought in that twelve years later, the city still had problems caused by the inflation. (Their own money was almost worthless.)

When Musa returned to Mali he brought many new people. Especially important were Moslem scholars. One was an architect, Al Saheli of Cordoba, who built a beautiful palace and a university in Timbuktu. Now even more people came to Mali—traders, religious leaders, and scholars.

Mansa Musa had hoped to return to Mecca and leave the empire to his son, but the empire was so large and so much had to be done that once he returned he never had a chance to leave again. In 1337 Mansa Kankan Musa died, leaving his son, Maghan, to rule the great empire of Mali.

Student Activity
International Biographies
Book 1
Lesson 8, Handout 24
Sample

Name____________________

Date ____________________

Trade in Ancient Mali

The Arabs used camels in the dry African climate in preference to donkeys or horses. They traveled in large caravans with each camel carrying about 300 pounds of trade goods. When they came to the Niger River, they brought slabs of salt to trade for gold. Today Mali mines bauxite (aluminum ore) and iron as well as gold. Millet, rice, peanuts, and cotton are grown. What do you think they might trade today? Load your camel on the next page.

Name________________________

Date ________________________

My Camel Is Ready to Join the Caravan

Queen Nefertiti

Objectives

- To recognize Queen Nefertiti as a queen of ancient Egypt
- To identify characteristics of Queen Nefertiti
- To recognize and list personal qualities unique to each student

Notes to the Teacher

Queen Nefertiti, wife of Akhenaten IV, (Amenhotep, original name) lived in ancient Egypt. She is most famous for her beauty and her loyalty to her husband. Many statues and paintings of her have been unearthed in the Nile Valley region. She and her husband are credited with initiating a belief in one god or monotheistic religion. After disputes with the priests and wisemen of that day, Nefertiti and Akhenaten left Cairo to found the divine city of "Armana." They found inspiration in the god "Aten" the Sun god. Since Nefertiti and Akhenaten were considered to be divine, many statues and paintings were made in their image and that of their six daughters. Nefertiti held a high government position. Egyptian women were not considered to be equal with men; they were not allowed opinions, to own property, make decisions, and certainly not to worship the gods. The fact that Nefertiti did participate alone and with her husband demonstrates her independence and courage. She was a forerunner of the modern woman.

This lesson focuses on Nefertiti as a woman loved by her people not only for her physical beauty but also for the beauty she had within. Students discuss her characteristics and the values she lived by which are still important today. After analyzing Nefertiti, they can begin to look within and find qualities they have that make them special. Using **Handouts 27** and **28,** students list adjectives and some nouns that describe or relate to Nefertiti and to themselves. The handouts can also be used to record characteristics of other important women or men. Displaying the handouts in the classroom can be a reminder to students of their positive qualities.

INTERDISCIPLINARY STRANDS:
Art, English/Language Arts, Geography, History, Math

MATERIALS:
Handouts 26, **27**, and **28**, pencil or pen, poster board, markers or crayons, prizes for pyramid winners (optional), world wall map

TERMS:
archaeological, Aten, divine, heretic, monotheistic

Resources

Aldred, Cyril. *Akhenaten, King of Egypt*. London: Thomas and Hudson Ltd. Inc. 1988.

Burt, Olive W. *Black Women of Valor,* illustrator Paul Frame. New York: Julian Messner, a division of Simon and Schuster, 1974.

David, Rosalie. *Cult of the Sun: Myth and Magic in Ancient Egypt*. London: J.M. Dent, 1980.

Garber, Janet Serlin editor. *The Concise Encyclopedia of Ancient Civilizations*. Grolier of Canada Ltd., 1975.
Harris, Geraldine. *Ancient Egypt*. New York: Facts on File Publications, 1990.
Holmes, Burnham. *Nefertiti, the Mystery Queen*. New York: Contemporary Perspectives, distributed by Raintree Publisher, 1977.
Santoro, Christopher. *Ancient Egypt,* illustrator Daniel Cohen. New York: Doubleday, 1989.
Sertima, Ivan Van editor. *Egypt Revisited: Journal of African Civilizations*. New Brunswick: Transaction Publications, 1989.
Wells, Evelyn. *Nefertiti.* Garden City, New York: Doubleday 1964.

Procedure

1. Show a picture of the Nefertiti bust pictured at the beginning of **Handout 26**. Ask if anyone knows who it is or the country of origin of the statue. It is so famous that some students may know it or recognize it as Egyptian. If none do, tell them it is a statue of the Egyptian, Queen Nefertiti. Explain that the gold necklace was like a collar and was set with precious jewels. The links were petal-shaped and showed her love for nature and flowers. There was a snake emblem representing supreme power on her blue headdress. Under the headdress her skull may have been shaven for it was the practice for both Egyptian men and women to shave their heads for comfort from the desert heat. Wigs were worn in public and it is known that Nefertiti wore one.

2. Read the biography of Nefertiti in **Handout 26**.

3. Locate Egypt, Armana, and Cairo on a world wall map. Explain that an ancient civilization grew in this area along the Nile River.

4. Lead a discussion focusing on Nefertiti's unique religious beliefs and her role in Egyptian society. Urge students to use adjectives to describe her.

5. Distribute **Handout 27**. Tell students to unscramble the words which are all descriptive of Nefertiti, then to fill in the pyramid, matching numbers in the boxes to the number of letters in each word. For each correct answer, they should add the total letter count. *(Left column answers: Ahkenaten, Aten, beautiful, Armana, queen, equal; Right column answers: monotheistic, independent, black, Egypt, divine.)*

6. Have students share their answers, define each word, and tell how each is related to Nefertiti. Afterwards, each person should count up the total points that they earned. You may wish to have a prize or reward for the most correct answers.

7. Distribute **Handout 28**. Have students complete the pyramid by writing words that describe themselves. These words should reflect positive characteristics. Students may wish to design an Egyptian background on the handout when they are finished.

8. An alternative is to have students choose a person whose values they admire, and complete the pyramid for that person. Some suggestions are George Bush, Anwar Sadat, Martin Luther King, etc.

9. Display the pyramids on poster board. Students can shape the paper to form an actual pyramid to place on their desks.

Enrichment/Extension

1. Research and write reports on other African queens. (See Appendix, **Handout 45**.)

2. Research other strong and independent women such as Winnie Mandela, Coretta Scott King, Cleopatra, Susan B. Anthony, Queen Elizabeth I, and Golda Meir. Perform a role play showing an event from their lives.

3. Research and discuss the differences between monotheistic and polytheistic religions. Prepare an illustrated chart showing the differences.

4. Visit the Egyptian section of the local art museum. Draw a picture showing a favorite or interesting artifact.

5. Other potential lessons relating to Nefertiti and ancient Egypt can be found in "King Tut," *World Cultures / World History* (Villa Maria, Pa.: Center for Learning, 1988).

Art Notation

Nefertiti's portrait depicts her as she appears in the famous statue which was unearthed in Egypt. Many people recognize this striking young queen but do not know the role she played in Egypt's history. She was more than just "another pretty face!" (see Appendix, **Handout 58**.)

Student Activity
International Biographies
Book 1
Lesson 9, Handout 26 (page 1)
Sample

Name________________________

Date ________________________

Nefertiti

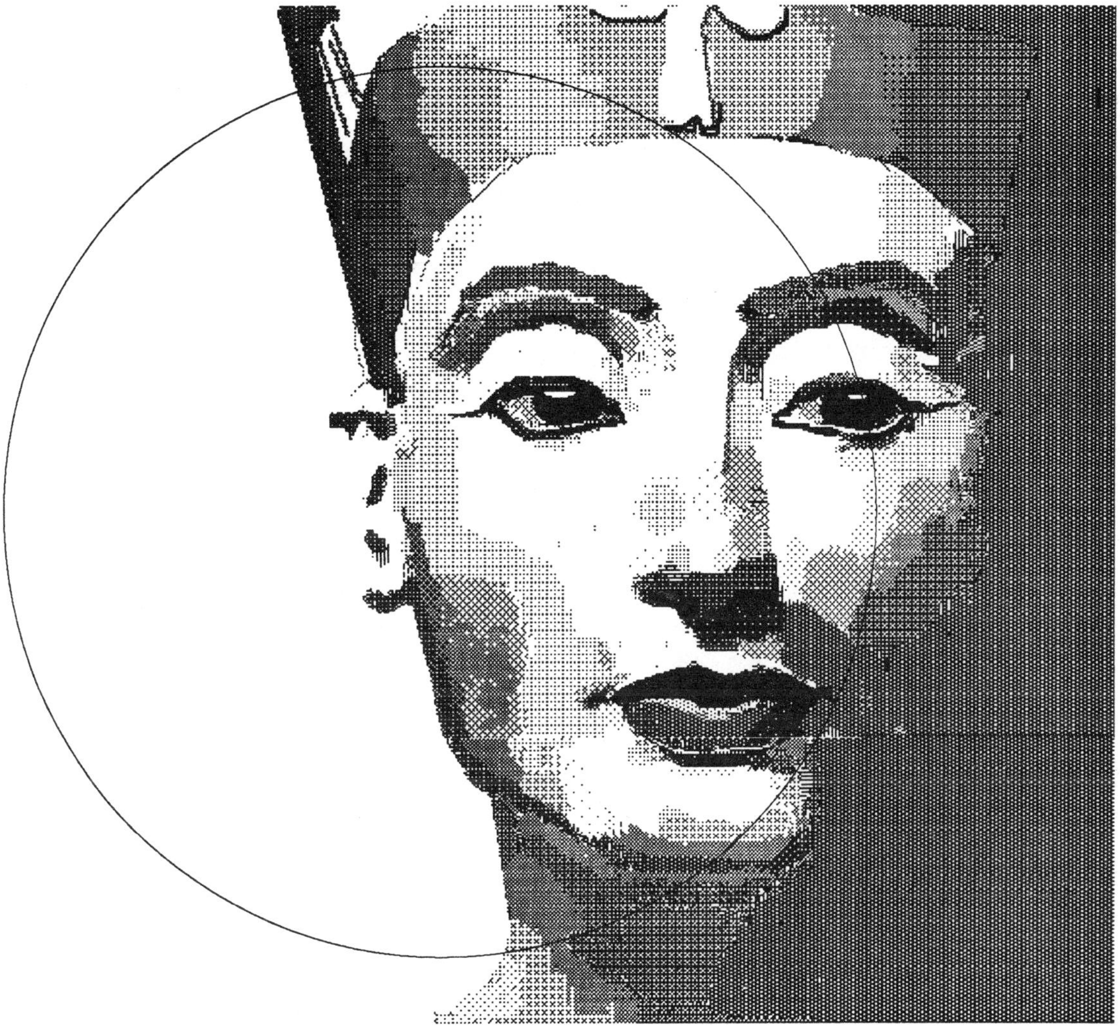

It was a hot afternoon in Armana, Egypt on December 6, 1912. The European in charge of the expedition, Professor Ludwig Borchardt, was inside taking a rest out of the sun. The Egyptian workmen continued to work under the direction of Mohammed Ahmes EsSenussi, the foreman of the archaeological dig, who worked with them.

Name____________________

Date ____________________

As he lifted another shovel of sand, EsSenussi caught sight of a golden flesh-colored fragment in the sand. He cried out and raised his hand to stop the digging. The workmen ran to the place where he was working. They, too, saw the gleam of something in the sand. A dirt-carrier was sent to Professor Borchardt's tent immediately.

He came at a trot despite the heat. He knelt at the spot his foreman indicated and with "trained, sensitive fingertips, with reverent breath, Professor Borchardt moved the sand from the buried object, grain by grain."[1] He grew increasingly excited as the object was revealed and, along with his workers, gasped in wonder and delight as the life-sized head of a beautiful woman appeared.

"It was Nefertiti, destined to become the most celebrated, copied, and admired bust in the world, the most famous face of all the Egyptian queens."[2]

Who was Nefertiti and how did this famous bust come to be buried in the sands of Egypt?

Nefertiti was the wife of King Akhenaten IV of ancient Egypt. They grew up together in the capital city of Thebes and lived in the royal palace of King Amenhotep II. At that time Egypt was the greatest and richest civilization in the world. Atkenaten was the king's first-born and only son and Nefertiti was Atkenaten's favorite companion. The two children played in the palace and along the banks of the Nile River overlooking the kingdom they would one day rule.

In 1372 B.C. Akhenaten became co-ruler with his father. He and Nefertiti prepared to assume their duties as king and queen. She would be wife, priestess, and hostess, and she would be required to be faithful, beautiful, and charming.

Great attention was paid to the personal appearance of royal ladies in Egypt. Dozens of attendants took care of Nefertiti. "There was a supervisor of the bath, a first lady of the eye pencil, a keeper of perfumes, a guardian of the jewel box, a tender of the oil jars. Tweezers, combs, scissors, kohl sticks, rouge pot and eye pencil, eye paint, eyewashes, depilatories, razors for shaving the head, pins, needles, hands mirrors of

[1]Evelyn Wells, *Nefertiti* (Garden City, N.Y.: Doubleday and Company, Inc., 1964), 8.
[2]Ibid.

Name____________________

Date ____________________

highly polished silver, gold, or bronze with handles shaped like animals, people or gods—all had their guardians."[3]

When Akhenaten turned sixteen, he became king in his own right. He and Nefertiti were married and she became queen of Egypt. The young king had an inquiring mind and studied and questioned many of the laws and beliefs of the Egyptian people. The Egyptians worshipped many gods. They believed the earth was their mother, the sun their father, and every living creature, rock, and tree held the spirit of a god. There were over 2000 different gods and goddesses, each with special powers. Akhenaten searched for the meaning of the gods and came to believe in one god—the sun god—Aten.

Akhenaten and Nefertiti wanted to change the Egyptian religion to belief in one god. This began a period called "the revolution of Armana." The royal priests were against the idea of one god for they controlled the wealth of the country and were in the top government positions. Belief in one god meant that they would lose their power. But Akenaten and Nefertiti persisted in their belief and decided to leave Thebes and create a new city.

They named the new city Armana. Beautiful temples and palaces were built, but they did not want material wealth to be all that mattered. They enjoyed nature and beauty and encouraged the seeking of truth. In the new city there was freedom of expression. Poets, writers, artists, and sculptors flocked there. Nefertiti was immortalized by countless pictures, statues, and murals that showed her beauty and Akhenaten's deep love for her. The Egyptian people worshipped Akhenaten and Nefertiti and believed they could send prayers to the god, Aten, through them.

But this beautiful city was left uncompleted and abandoned in less than twenty years. The Egyptian people were not ready to abandon their belief in many gods. Enemies plotted against the royal couple and called them heretics and rebels. Akhenaten grew ill and a strickened and sad Nefertiti nursed him through his last days. When he died, their nine-year-old son became king. For awhile, Nefertiti, helped her son, King Tutankhamen, rule Egypt and fought to hold their dream of one god for Egypt. But again, her enemies prevailed and the priests persuaded the young pharaoh to move the capital city back to Thebes.

[3]Ibid., 65.

Name________________________

Date ________________________

Nefertiti remained at Armana. Tutankhamen (famous in modern times as King Tut) died a few years later, and the last glimpse of Nefertiti is in the magnificent palace at Armana fiercely remaining faithful to the worship of one god, Aten and to the memories of her beloved husband, Akhenaten.

Just twenty years after it was built, the city of Armana was destroyed. The beautiful palaces were razed to the ground and the statues and artwork crushed. Their enemies tried to destroy all traces of Akhenaten and Nefertiti. But four thousands years later, her statue reappeared in the dust of an archaeological dig, and the memories of a woman who was admired for her beauty, courage, loyalty, and independence once more gained the attention of the world.

Student Activity
International Biographies
Book 1
Lesson 9, Handout 27

Name________________________

Date ________________________

Nefertiti's Pyramid

Below are words relating to Nefertiti, queen of Egypt. Unscramble the words and write your answer on the line. Count the number of letters in each word. Find that number on the pyramid and put the words into the correct layer.

enkahenat ____________________

ntea ____________________

teabulfui ____________________

naarma ____________________

neqeu ____________________

lueqa ____________________

themotnoisic ____________________

pendentedni ____________________

ckbla ____________________

tpegy ____________________

niveid ____________________

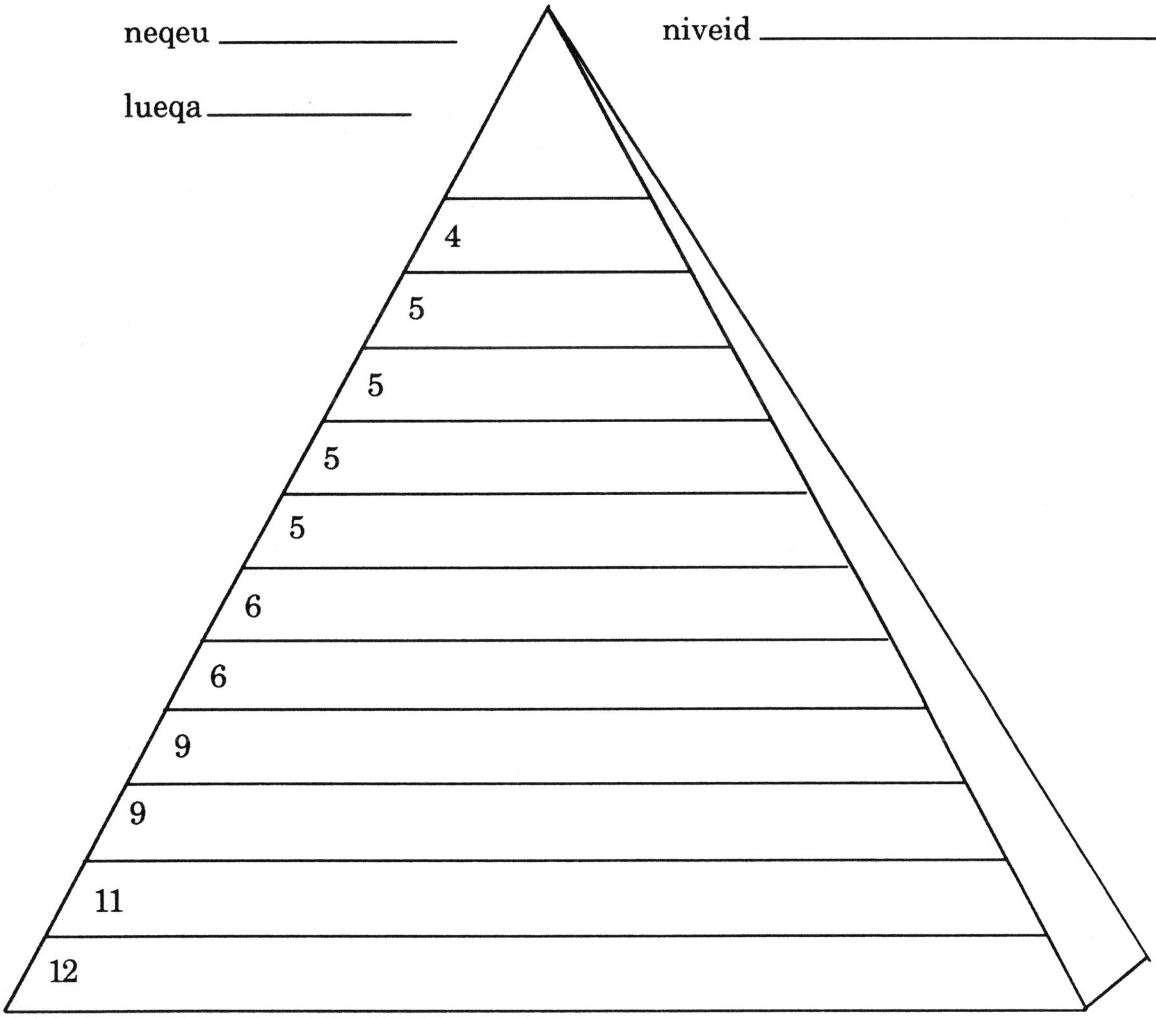

Name________________________

Date ________________________

Pyramid

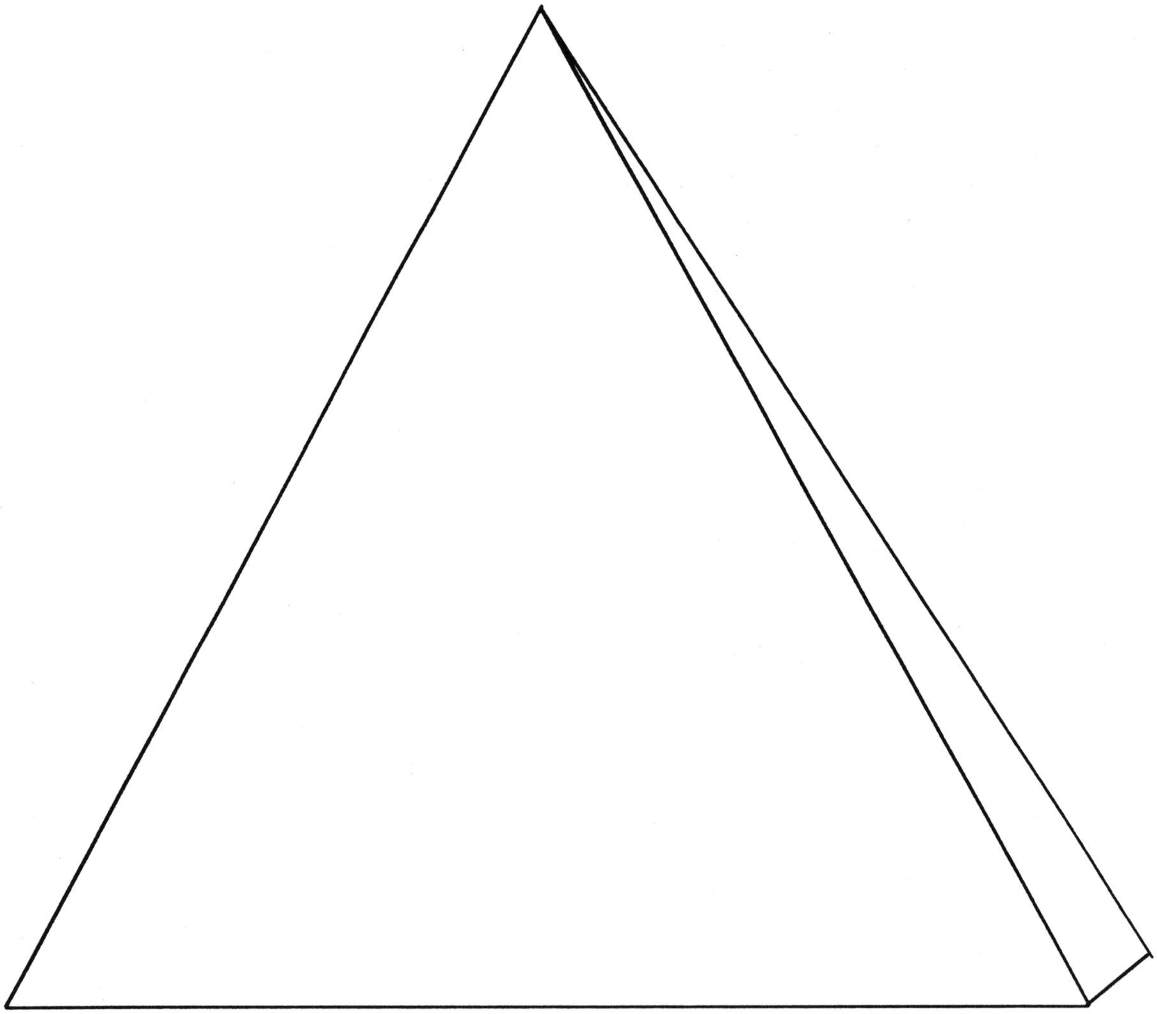

Julius Nyerere

Objectives

- To identify Julius Nyerere and his contributions to the independence of Tanzania
- To create an illustrated map of Tanzania

Notes to Teacher

Have available pictures and books about the country of Tanzania so students can see what the geographic environment of the area is and how the people adapt to this region.

When introducing Julius Nyerere's biography, tell students that the Zanaki pronounciation of his name is Nyuh-reh-reh, but that others pronounce it Nyuh-reh-ree. Emphasize that this man was the single-most important individual in helping Tanzania gain independence. Make students aware that the struggle is not over. Tanzania still has a poor agricultural economy that is dependent on foreign countries for its income. The per capita income of Tanzanians is only a little over $200 per year. Swahili is their national language.

In this lesson students read Nyerere's biography and discuss how he helped Tanzania gain independence. In the activity students use maps to explore the geography of Tanzania and create an illustrated map that shows special features of the country.

INTERDISCIPLINARY SATRANDS:
Art, English/Languge Arts, Geography, History

MATERIALS:
Handouts 29, 30, and **31**, crayons or markers

TERMS:
colony, elders, independence, lore, mutiny

Resources

Haskins, Jim. *Count Your Way Through Africa.* Minneapolis: Carolrhoda Books Inc., 1989.
McCulla, Patricia E. *Tanzania.* New York: Chelsea House Publishers, 1989.
McGraw Hill Encyclopedia of World Biography. New York: McGraw Hill Book Co., 1973, vol. 8, 162–165.
Smith, William Edgett. *We Must Run While They Walk.* New York: Random House, 1971.

Procedure

1. Teach students how to count to ten in Swahili. Tell them that this language developed between the Africans on the east coast and the Arab traders who came to do business. Explain that many countries on the east coast of Africa chose Swahili as their national language after independence.

Pronunciation Guide

1. /moja/MO-jah	5. /tano/TAH-no	8. /nane/NAH-nay
2. /mbili/mm-BEE-lee	6. /sita/SEE-tah	9. /tisa/TEE-sah
3. /tatu/TAH-too	7. /saba/SAH-bah	10. /kumi/KOO-mee
4. /nne/NN-Nay		

2. Introduce Julius Nyerere as a leader of Tanzania, a country on the east coast of Africa. Locate Tanzania on a world wall map. Also locate Zanzibar and Tanganyika and explain that these two countries combined to form Tanzania.

3. Show pictures of the country, people, and animals who live there. Discuss why such a big, diverse country would be difficult to modernize.

4. Ask students to tell if Nyerere did a good job in creating a modern African country. Have them explain their answers. What things do they think would improve their situation? Why?

5. Distribute **Handout 30**. Ask students to look at the map and discuss what kinds of things they would put on a pictorial map of Tanzania. Encourage them to research to include as many things as possible on their maps *(Agricultural and industrial products, people, places, animals, etc.)*.

6. On **Handout 31** have students sketch in pictures. Encourage them to be accurate about the kinds of things they include. Have them color their pictures. (If students have magazines available they can do a collage-type map by cutting out pictures of animals and people and gluing them to their map.)

7. Mount their maps on poster board or redraw them using their sketches as rough drafts and copy a good draft on the poster board and color it.

8. Stage a show-and-tell and have students explain what their maps contain and why. Display the maps.

Enrichment/Extension

1. Create a salt map of Tanzania and using food colors add additional features and labels to the map.

2. Research the Masai or some of the other tribal people of Tanzania to discover the special cultures in that country.

3. Research the kinds of agricultural and industrial products produced in Tanzania and determine their worth to the country's economic base.

4. Learn other Swahili words or words from other African languages. Make a picture book illustrating the African words.

5. Other potential lessons relating to Tanzania can be found in "Africa Emergent: A Discovery Exercise," *World History, Book 4*: 1920–1985 (Villa Maria, Pa.: The Center for Learning, 1986).

Art Notation

Julius Nyerere's portrait depicts him as a determined forceful personality. The two halves of a circle in the background represent the countries of Tanganyika and Zanzibar which he united as the country of Tanzania. (See Appendix, **Handout 58**.)

Name______________________

Date ______________________

Julius Nyerere

It was raining so hard that the women had a difficult time getting to fifteen-year old Mugaya's hut, but it was not long after their arrival that the sound of the newborn baby filled the air. There was great rejoicing because the baby was a boy. He was called Kambarage because of the hard rains that fell that March day in 1922, a name honoring the ancient spirit who lived in the rain. Kambarage was the second of Mugaya's eight children.

Name________________________

Date ________________________

In the tribal lore of the Zanaki, their group had been started by a rainmaker who had failed to make it rain and had been forced to move to an area southeast of Lake Victoria in Tanganyika years before. (The Zanaki are the smallest tribe of the 126 tribes in the country.)

There had been no chief in this tribe until the Germans took control of Tanganyika in the middle 1800s. Before, they were run by the warriors of the tribe with the abagambi (speakers for the tribe) warning the warriors what might happen if certain actions were taken. The speakers had no power except in their ability to convince the warriors that their point of view was the correct choice. When the Germans arrived, they insisted that the Zanaki needed a chief to be in charge.

The Germans picked a chief, but he did not last long. His cousin Nyerere Burito, Kambarage Nyerere's father, was then made chief. He was sixty-one when Kambarage was born. The name Nyerere means caterpillar and was given to his father because when he was born in 1860, there had been a terrible plague of caterpillars that destroyed the area in which the Zanaki tribe lived.

After World War I the Germans were forced to give up their claim to Tanganyika and the British took control of the colony. The new rulers were most disturbed that Nyerere Burito had twenty-two wives. This was a common practice in Africa, but the British did not understand that the Africans needed many wives to work the farmland to produce food for their families.

The price of a good Zanaki bride was about twenty cows. When Nyerere died in 1942, he left a total of twenty-six children. Even Kambarage's half-brother Edward had eleven wives, but Kambarge told him he would be better off to buy a tractor instead of a wife to do the work. Edward just laughed at this idea.

Until he was twelve, Kambarage rarely saw Europeans or Asians around his homeland. He grew up as all children did in the tribe, fearing their powerful Masai neighbors with whom they frequently had to battle with their bows and arrows. Their weapons were no match for the Masai spears. The Zanaki had learned a trick to beat them, however. They would fire their arrows into the air and the Masai would lift their large shields high to prevent being hit. While their shields were raised the Zanaki fired more arrows into the lower parts of their bodies. This proved to be an excellent plan, and they were able to defeat the Masai!

Name________________________

Date ________________________

Kambarage was twelve years old when he went to a school twenty-six miles away. Soon after he went to school, Chief Nyerere bought him a bride. The chief was getting old and knew that he must provide for Kambarage before he died. He knew that Kambarage would be inherited by a brother or an uncle and that if he did not arrange the bridal purchase, Kambarage might never be able to marry because inherited sons are the last to get money for a bride. (Kambarage never married the girl his father had paid cows for because he met Maria Gabriel and married her instead.)

Kambarage was an outstanding student. He quickly learned Swahili and English and scored first in the territorial examination given in 1936. He moved on to a secondary school at Musoma where he was required to attend religious services twice a week. Even though he was a tribal child he went along with a friend to instructions in the Catholic faith. When he was twenty, he was baptized a Catholic and changed his name to Julius.

In school Julius sometimes got into trouble for defending classmates against rules that he believed to be unfair. When he finished his schooling, he taught biology and history at St. Mary's School. He also became the secretary of the Tanganyika African Association. His job invoved checking for storekeepers who overcharged on items that were under price controls after World War II. He quit this job when one of the store owners he caught had his case dropped. Julius was very angry because nothing had been done to punish the man.

In 1949 he went to Edinburgh, Scotland to study history and economics. He hoped to learn about politics and government and return home to help his country gain independence.

He met Maria Gabriel at Edinburgh and wanted to marry her, but she wanted him to prove that his education had not changed him. A year passed until his wedding, and he made preparations for it. He built a house for them, and he took off his English shoes and with his bare feet mixed the sand and cement for the house. This earned Maria's respect, and they were married January 24, 1953.

Nyerere was one of only a few Africans in Tanganyika who had an advanced western education. He reorganized TANU (Tanganyika African National Union) and became its president. He spent so much time with the group, he had to resign his teaching position. Little money was available, but he kept up the fight for independence by addresssing the United

Name_______________________

Date _______________________

Nations several times to discuss independence from the British. He was finally asked by the British to head the legislative committee for the country. In 1960 TANU people were elected to seventy of seventy-one seats in the legislature, and Nyerere became the first African to be chief minister in Tanganyika.

Independence came on December 9, 1961. Nyerere resigned his job as chief minister and was elected as Tanganyika's first president. It became a republic on December 9, 1962. As president he used the motto, "Uhuru na Kaza" (freedom and work) to describe his policies. He wanted to eliminate the three big enemies of his people: poverty, ignorance, and disease. He believed that his country had to stop depending on other countries for their needs and became economically independent.

His biggest problem occurred when the army mutinied because they wanted more pay and more African officers. Zanzibar, a nearby island country also had a revolution. Nyerere went into hiding for a short time, and when he reappeared he was able to settle the problems by giving higher wages to the army and uniting Zanzibar with Tanganyika to form the republic of Tanzania.

Nyerere wanted his country to become a part of the modern world and he battled African tradition and the effects of European colonization. He stepped down from the presidency in 1985, but Tanzania today is still working toward his goal of modernization—a government that is fair to all and a safe, healthy, and prosperous environment in which to live and work. A generation from now its success may be judged.

Student Activity
International Biographies
Book 1
Lesson 10, Handout 30
Sample

Name_______________________

Date _______________________

Tanzania

This map shows where important cities and bodies of water are located in Tanzania. On **Handout 31**, highlight some of the special features of this country. For example: draw some of its wildlife on the Serengeti Plain, for its candelabra cactus, an Arab Dhow (sailing ship), a Masai warrior, etc. Place the pictures in the correct locations.

Fig. 10.1

Fig. 10.1. Patricia E. McCulla, *Places and People of the World: Tanzania* (New York: Chelsea House, 1989), 7,8.

Name______________________

Date ______________________

My Pictorial Map of Tanzania

Alan Paton

Objectives

- To identify Alan Paton and his role in the fight against apartheid in South Africa
- To produce a slogan to protest social injustice

Notes to the Teacher

A review of the history of South Africa is helpful to students relative to this lesson. Students need to know what is meant by minority and majority rule and about the system of apartheid. A reference sheet is provided that gives a brief history of South Africa.

Students should also be made aware that some of the injustices of apartheid are beginning to change due to public and economic pressures that have been applied by other countries. Alan Paton helped make the world aware of the social injustices prevalent in South Africa through the publication of his novel, *Cry, The Beloved Country*. He had fought the system before the anti-apartheid fight became popular. Today, he continues to lead his party in the fight against injustice.

Students read his biography and discuss the effects of apartheid and the effects of a novel about discrimination on the attitude of world society. They then design a bumper sticker that expresses their view on apartheid.

INTERDISCIPLINARY STRANDS:
Art, English/Language Arts, Geography, History, Literature

MATERIALS:
Handouts 32, 33, and 34, reference page on South Africa, markers, world wall map

TERMS:
Afrikaners, apartheid, delinquent, enteric fever, novel, penitentiaries, racism, reforms

Resources

Mack, John. *Zulus.* Morristown, N.J.: Silver Burdett, 1980.
McKenna, Nancy Durrell. *A Zulu Family.* Minneapolis: Lerner Publications, 1984.
Paton, Alan. *Cry the Beloved Country.* New York: Charles Scribner's Sons, 1948.
Paton, Alan. *Journey Continued.* New York: Charles Scribner's Sons, 1988.
Paton, Alan. *The Land and People of South Africa.* Philadelphia: Lippincott, 1972.
Paton, Jonathan. *The Land and People of South Africa.* New York: Lippincott, 1990.
Paton, Alan. *Towards the Mountain.* New York: Charles Scribner's Sons, 1980.
Rochman, Hazel (selected by). *Somehow Tenderness Survives: Stones of Southern Africa.* New York: Harper & Row, 1988.
Watson, R. L. *South Africa in Pictures.* Minneapolis: Lerner Publications, Co., 1988.

Procedure

1. Show pictures of South Africa's beauty—the countryside homes, farms. Then show pictures of black South African homelands. Discuss why these differences exist.

2. Discuss briefly the history of South Africa and difficulties between the English, the Afrikaners, the coloreds, and the Africans. Continue by researching in recent news magazine articles about the government of South Africa and the recent events there. Use the Reference page. It can be used as an optional handout.

3. Locate South Africa on a world wall map. Discuss the natural resources that are found there. Also locate Pietermaritzburg, Natal, and Johannesburg.

4. Introduce Alan Paton as a man who is fighting the system of apartheid. Read **Handout 32**, the biography of Paton. Discussion should include the influence of his upbringing on Paton's attitudes, beliefs, and values as an adult. *(It influenced him greatly.)* Emphasis should be placed on his early entry into the currently popular anti-apartheid fight.

5. Divide the class into groups of five. (See Appendix, **Handout 48.**) Ask each group to think of at least three reasonable ideas about ways the Africans could gain their civil rights.

6. Reconvene the class and lists their ideas on the chalkboard or on an overhead transparency. Rank order according to what might work the best.

7. Distribute **Handouts 33 and 34**. Examine the sample in **Handout 33**. Then tell students to use **Handout 34** to create a bumper sticker with a slogan (three to five words) that speaks against apartheid. Have them write their slogan neatly with markers and decorate the sticker.

8. Display the bumper stickers with a map of South Africa and current news articles about the country.

Enrichment/Extension

1. Write letters to the president of South Africa explaining why you feel South Africa should end the apartheid system. Share any responses with the class.

2. Write a short story that is fiction but deals with real issues about a current social problem—world hunger, the destruction of our environment, hopelessness, or another issue. Share the stories with the class.

3. Read *Cry, The Beloved Country* by Alan Paton. Form groups to discuss the significance of the book. An additional resource is the *Curriculum Unit: Cry, The Beloved Country* (Villa Maria, Pa.: The Center for Learning, 1988).

4. Other potential lessons on South Africa and apartheid can be found in the following Center for Learning publications: "Apartheid," *World History, Book 4 1920–1986;* and "A Case Study: Apartheid vs. Human Rights," *Current Issues in Global Education* (Villa Maria, Pa.: 1988).

Art Notation

Alan Paton's portrait depicts him as a man caught between two worlds. His serious and intent expression might indicate that he is pondering the fates of the two South Africas he knows, loves, and writes about. (See Appendix, **Handout 58.**)

Reference Page

South Africa Historical Background

1600s
The Dutch East India Company settled near the Cape of Good Hope. The Germans and the French Huguenots came later. They produced a language that was a mixture of Dutch and other languages and it was called Afrikaans. These European farmers became known as "Boers."

1814
Great Britain sent settlers. The Boers began to move into the interior. Those who moved were called Trekkers.

1870s
Diamonds and gold were discovered.

1879
Native African tribes revolted. Zulu army was defeated and the Xhosa fell.

1899–1902
The Boer War: The British defeated the Boers and controlled the Transvaal, the Orange Free State, and Natal. This area became the Union of South Africa, 1910.

1924–1939
James Barry Hertzog was Prime Minister and headed the Nationalist Party. He reduced the voting rights of the nonwhites and set up reserved lands for black Africans.

1948
Daniel F. Malan, Nationalist Party, became Prime Minister. The practice of apartheid became the official policy of South Africa. *Cry, The Beloved Country* was published.

1960–1970s
Racial conflict was the result of the apartheid policy.

1980s
"Independent Homelands" were formed for black ethnic groups.

1984
Bishop Desmond Tutu won the Nobel Peace Prize for trying nonviolent methods to solve South Africa's problems.

1990s
What is happening in South Africa today?

[1]Adapted from *Barron's Book Notes, Alan Paton's Cry, The Beloved Country* by Rose Sallberg Kam (Woodbury, N.Y.: Barron's Educational Series Inc., 1985), 22–29.

Name________________________

Date ________________________

Alan Paton

The year is 1948 . . . "Good-bye, Daddy. Good-bye, Daddy.," were the last words he heard as he headed down the dusty road. Those were his children, he thought, and he had to leave them behind each month after his visit. How he missed them, but he could not take them to Johannesburg. Families were not allowed. The apartheid system of government in South Africa had strict rules for the native Africans who lived there. The white minority had complete control and they made all the rules. How he wished for things to be different. He had heard recently that a white man, Alan Paton, was on their side. Who was this man and why had he told the real story of the South African tragedy called apartheid?

Name________________________

Date ________________________

Alan Paton is an author who wrote a book in 1948 about South Africa and the injustice of the apartheid system of racism. It is a novel—but the story of the racism and the sadness in such a beautiful country is real. His book is called *Cry, the Beloved Country*.

Alan Paton was born in Pietermaritzburg in the province of Natal, South Africa, on January 11, 1903. His father was a Scotsman who worked as a court reporter, and his mother, a teacher, was of English descent. He was the eldest of their four children.

Alan was brought up in a strict Christian home where there was no drinking or swearing. He learned neither prejudice nor the cruel words used to speak of the Africans or the Afrikaners (the descendants of the original Dutch settlers who were disliked by the British).

His father ran a household in which he used the cane and paddle when he was not obeyed. Alan was afraid of his father and so was his brother, but they still occasionally disobeyed him. One winter day they were made to wear an undershirt to school which they hated; so when they got out of sight of the house, they took the shirts off and hid them in the bushes. When they returned from school, they stopped and picked them up. They never got caught but it would have meant a whipping if they had.

When he was six he entered school—a girls' school. All young boys did the same, but Alan was timid and afraid everyone would think he was a sissy. The older boys did pick on him going back and forth to school. They even got him into trouble when they made him push a little girl off the path onto the ground. He ran home and she said nothing, but the next day he was called into the principal's office and given a punishment. He had to eat at the girls' table for the next week!

Alan moved on to a boys' school at an early age, and he remained the youngest in his class for the rest of his school years because he advanced early two more times. He liked to read and write poetry, a habit which he continued throughout his life.

When he finished high school, there was no money from home to help him attend college, but at that time the government was offering to pay for the education of those who would like to be teachers. Alan accepted this funding and began his studies to prepare for teaching. He made

Name____________________

Date ____________________

several life-long friends in college. While in college he wrote two novels, but he tore them up. He continued to write poetry.

After he graduated, he taught in private schools for the sons of rich white South Africans. At Ixopo he met his wife-to-be, Dorrie. They were later married and had two boys Jonathan and Donald.

Paton became very ill from enteric fever when he was about thirty years old. He took a long time recovering and while he was resting, he had a chance to think about his life. He knew that he did not want to spend the rest of it teaching rich boys.

When he recovered fully, he took a job as principal of Diepkloof Reformatory in Johannesburg. The reformatory housed black African boys from age seven to twenty-one who were declared by the courts to be delinquent. It was a terrible place when he arrived—all behind a barbed—wire type fence. It was dirty and the facilities were not adequate to meet the needs of the boys.

Nineteen thirty-four was a time in South Africa when some reforms were being made. Some believed that the boys should be educated to help prepare them for the time when they would be released. He and Dorrie and their two sons spent ten years making changes that improved the reformatory, the staff, and living conditions. The people at the office of the Ministry of Education backed Paton's ideas. Some of the Afrikaners began to make noise, though, about this "gentle" treatment of black delinquents and tried to stop him.

Alan Paton wanted to know more about reforms in the rest of the world and was able to get funding to visit penitentiaries in Europe and North America. He spent a long time in the United States visiting places on both the east and west coasts. He made new friends along the way and got an idea of what had been done with prisoners of all ages.

While Alan Paton sailed across the Atlantic and while he was in his hotel rooms in strange countries, he wrote the story that was to become his first published novel.

It was released in the United States in 1948. Word of it had also begun to reach his home in South Africa. Paton was thrilled at the reception of his book which was later made into a play and then a film—an unsuccessful film from which he made very little money.

Name______________________

Date ______________________

Paton returned home and decided to leave the reformatory and retire to become a full-time writer. But a change occured in the South African government. The Nationalist Party, the Afrikaners, gained control of the government. They began to make the practice of apartheid a grim reality. People (mainly Africans) were being moved from their houses to areas away from the cities called homelands. More laws were passed to keep blacks and whites separated. This policy was called apartheid.

Paton was very unhappy and tried, along with his liberal, anti-nationalist friends, to stop this movement. His books and poetry spoke of some of the social injustices, and he founded a new political party called the Liberal Party of South Africa. This group continued to speak out against apartheid. Alan Paton testified in defense of Nelson Mandela, a leader of the anti-apartheid movement, at Mandela's trial.

Until his death in 1988, Paton continued to fight for justice for all in South Africa, hopeful that someday all of his countrymen and women would be treated with fairness and equality.

Student Activity
International Biographies
Book 1
Lesson 11, Handout 33
Sample

Name________________________

Date ________________________

Anti-Apartheid Bumper Sticker

Alan Paton wrote about the injustice of the apartheid system in South Africa. His work let people all around the world know the problems faced by black Africans. Here is a sample of a bumper sticker about this kind of injustice. See if you can make up a slogan with three to five words on it that also speaks against apartheid.

Name________________________

Date ________________________

My Anti-Apartheid Bumper Sticker

Anwar Sadat

Objective

- To identify Anwar Sadat as a leader of Egypt and a peacemaker in the Middle East
- To examine the decision-making process
- To role play making decisions

Notes to the Teacher

Anwar Sadat was the President of Egypt for eleven years until his assassination in 1981. He is remembered as a man of peace for his efforts to stop the war between the Arab nations and Israel. A brief overview of the Arab/Israeli conflict may help students better understand Sadat's role as peacemaker. The Resource Sheet included before the handouts can serve as an outline for the history of the conflict. Sadat won the Nobel Peace Prize in 1978 for the peace agreement reached between himself and Menachem Begin of Israel. The stand he took for peace cost his country the trust and friendship of other Arab nations. They did not like the fact that Sadat formed an alliance with Israel without consulting other Arab countries. They were against signing any treaty with Israel. As a result, Egypt was thrown out of the Arab League and all official League loans were stopped. Egypt was alienated from the countries which were its neighbors. Egypt's only support came from the United States, thousands of miles away.

This lesson focuses on the fact that Sadat took a stand which cost him a great deal. He did this because he knew peace was important. Students read his biography and discuss his life and decision to seek peace with Israel. Students also face decisions each day which may cause them to lose friends or not look "cool." Being strong enough to stand by these decisions is something that is often difficult to do. Peer pressure is strong. The lesson offers a role play in which the students can put themselves in decision-making situations.

INTERDISCIPLINARY STRANDS:
Drama, English/Language Arts, Geography, History, Political Science

MATERIALS:
Handout 35, 36, 37, and **38,** pencil, pen, world wall map

TERMS:
Arab League, assassinated, betrayed, Islam, Koran, Nobel Peace Prize, peace treaty, Wattle

Resources

Aufderheide, Patricia. *Anwar Sadat.* New York: Chelsea House Publications, 1985.
Hirst, David and Benson, Irene. *Sadat.* Binghampton, New York: Vail Ballou Press Inc., 1981.
Sadat, Anwar. *In Search of Identity: An Autobiography.* New York: Harper and Row, 1978.
Sadat, Camelia. *My Father and I.* New York: Macmillan Press, 1985.
Sullivan, George. *Sadat—The Man Who Changed Mid-East History.* New York: Walker, 1981.

Procedure

1. Ask students what they would do in the following situation:
   You belong to a group of friends. The group wants to vandalize the home of a person who has done something against the group. You feel it would be better to talk to the person and solve the problem peacefully. Your friends disagree and say if you don't join them in "rolling" the person's house—you are out of the group. What do you do?

2. Introduce Anwar Sadat as a leader of Egypt who faced a similar situation.
   Read his biography in **Handout 35.**

3. Use a world wall map to locate the Arab nations of Egypt, Iran, Iraq, Saudi Arabia, Syria, and Lebanon. Also locate Israel. Explain that the Arab nations not only have location in common, but also share the Islamic faith, Arabic language, and a similar culturel. Briefly review the history of the Arab-Israeli conflict using the Resource Sheet as a guide.

4. Discuss the life of Anwar Sadat. Emphasize the stand Sadat took for peace. Talk about the fact that other Arab nations were against Egypt. Ask students how they would feel in a similar situation. Have them list qualities that describe Sadat *(courageous, religious, intelligent, a peacemaker, a leader, loyal, etc.)*.

5. Use **Handout 36** to further discuss Sadat's decision to seek peace. Note how the decision-making process is organized: a problem is stated, a possible solution given, pros and cons are listed, and a decision is made.

6. Inform students that they also face many difficult decisions. Brainstorm possible decision students of today face *(drugs, violence, peer pressure, cheating and stealing, etc.)*

7. Divide students into small groups. (See Appendix, **Handout 48.**) Have each groups look over the scenarios listed on **Handout 37**. Ask the groups to discuss the scenarios and to choose one they would like to further discuss. Have each group use **Handout 38** to and decide how they would handle the problem described in the scenario they chose.

8. Have students share their decisions with the class. Have groups role play their scenario and dramatize their solution.

Enrichment/Extension

1. Research and write a report on other Arab nations. (See Appendix, **Handout 45.**)

2. Visit the local city hall for a council meeting. Discover how government operates at the local level, how leaders compromise, and how decisions are made.

3. Search newspapers and news magazines for articles about the Arab-Israeli conflict. (See Appendix, **Handout 52.**) Share the articles orally with the class or arrange a bulletin board display centered around the articles.

4. Other potential lessons relating to the Arab/Israeli conflict can be found in the following Center for Learning publications: "The Middle East: Arena for Dispute," *Current Issues in Global Education* (Villa Maria, Pa., 1988); and "Focus on the Middle East," and "The Middle East and the Big L.I.E.–Editorial Cartoons on Lebanon, Iran, and Egypt," *World History, Book 4: 1920–1985* (Villa Maria, Pa., 1986).

Art Notation

Anwar Sadat's portrait depicts him in a business suit, the garb he wore as Egypt's President. His open inquiring expression and the encompassing arc are clues to his leadership style. (See Appendix, **Handout 58.**)

Resource Sheet

Arab-Israeli Conflict

Palestine is an area of the Middle East that has long been occupied by Arabs. Jerusalem, the capital of Palestine is a holy city of the Islamic faith. However, Palestine was also in ancient time, the homeland of the Jewish people and Jerusalem is also their holy city. It has been a long-held dream of the Jewish people to again have a homeland in their Holy Land, a homeland open to all the Jews of the world.

1930–1947—Palestine is controlled by the British. Persecution of Jews by the Nazis in Germany increases Jewish immigration to Palestine.

1947—The United Nations draw up a plan that divides Palestine between the Arabs and the Jews. The Jewish part is called Israel. Jerusalem is included in the Arab part as an international city.

1948—British control ends and war between the new nation of Israel and the Arab nations break out.

1949—Fighting ends with Israel taking over most of Arab territory.

1950–1956—Hundreds of thousands of Arabs flee Israeli territory. Many stay in refugee camps which become their permanent homes. Arab nations want Palestine back and there are frequent border incidents.

1956—The Soviet Union provides aid to Egypt to build up its military.

1957—Egypt internationalizes the Suez Canal and Israel invades the Sinai Peninsula. The United Nations force Israel to withdraw.

1957–1967—Arab commandos continue to attack Israeli settlements and Israel retaliates with their own raids.

1967—Six Day War in which Israel seized the remaining Arab territory in The Sinai Peninsula. The Suez Canal is left unpassable.

1970—The active Arab opposition becomes unified under the Palestine Liberation Organization. Extremist begin a worldwide campaign of terrorism against Israel.

1973—Egypt attacks Israel. Fighting is halted by a United Nation's cease fire.

1979—Egypt signs a peace treaty with Israel.

1980s —Israel and the Arab nations remain at peace, but there are frequent conflicts. Iran and Lebanon become centers of conflict in the Middle East.

1990s—What is currently happening in the Middle East?

Name_______________________

Date _______________________

Anwar Sadat

The child squirmed with excitement. This day had been full of wonder. Never had Nasser (Victory) City on the outskirts of Cairo seen such a day as this one—October 6, 1981.

Name______________________

Date ______________________

It began at 11:00 A.M. when President Anwar Sadat had taken his place in the reviewing stand. He was dressed in a splendid, colorful military uniform. He had arrived in a limousine with eight bodyguards!

After a brief reading from the Moslem holy book, the Koran, and a short speech thanking the Americans for new military equipment, President Sadat laid a wreath at the Tomb of the Unknown Soldier. Then, the military parade began. The procession was over ten miles long. At noon there was an exhibition of free-fall parachuting. Just as the child was getting a bit bored with the continuing parade, the air show started. Jets screamed overhead in the cloudless sky billowing red, blue, and green smoke. On the ground, the military parade continued and units towing heavy field guns crawled past the reviewing stand.

Everyone was looking upwards fascinated at the air show. Few noticed when one of the trucks stopped in front of the reviewing stand. Suddenly, a soldier raced from the truck toward the President. Three other men in the back of the truck lobbed hand grenades toward the reviewing stand. The stunned bodyguards and security people watched in horror as the first man leaned over the barrier and pumped automatic fire into the President at point-blank range.

Chaos erupted. The child and adults present realized something terrible had happened. Only later did they realize that they had been eyewitnesses to a tragic event—the assassination of Anwar Sadat.

Some people rejoiced that Anwar Sadat had been killed. They did not agree with his policies and thought him a villain. Others mourned the senseless killing of a man they regarded as a hero and wise leader. Who was Anwar Sadat and why did he inspire such strong emotions?

Anwar Sadat was President of Egypt from 1970 until he was assassinated in 1981. It is sad that Sadat, a great peacemaker, was killed during a celebration of war by soldiers in his own army. The soldiers and many other Arab people were against a peace treaty Sadat had signed with Israel. Egypt along with the other Arab nations of Saudi Arabia, Iran, Iraq, Syria, and Lebanon were united in one group called the Arab League. The Arabian people share the same language and religion. Their countries are near each other in the Middle East and together they had been fighting Israel since 1948. In that year, Israel was given land that Arabs had lived on. Since then, the Arabs and Israelis have been in conflict.

Name________________________

Date ________________________

Sadat did not agree with the other Arab Nations. Even though he knew that he would make enemies, he wanted peace. He hoped that peace with Israel and friendship with the United States would improve living conditions at home. In 1978 Sadat met with Menachem Begin, Prime Minister of Israel, and Jimmy Carter, President of the United States and signed a peace treaty. For his efforts he won the Nobel Peace prize. But the other Arab nations felt betrayed by Sadat's decision and decided to put Egypt out of the Arab League. They would no longer consider Egypt to be one of the Arab nations.

Sadat's courageous decision was typical of the man. He had made such decisions all his life. Sadat was born on December 25, 1918 in a mudbrick hut in the small village of Mit Abul Kom. As a boy he played along the fertile Nile delta that surrounded his village. His first teacher, a kindly Islamic clerk, taught him to read and instilled in him a deep and lasting faith in Islam. Even as an adult, Sadat had a dark mark on his forehead, the result of repeatedly touching his head to the ground in prayer.

As Sadat grew up, he became aware of the British presence in Egypt. He wanted his country freed of the troops Britain had in Egypt and of any control the British had in Egyptian government. Sadat joined the army and became part of a group of officers who wanted to revolt against the British. When World War II broke out, Sadat helped Germany against the British and was arrested and sent to prison. In 1944 he escaped and remained hidden until the end of the war. After the war, he again joined officers, under the leadership of Lieutenant Colonel Nasser in planning a revolt against the British. In 1952 the long-awaited uprising took place. The rebels took control of army headquarters, the British withdrew their troops from Egypt, and Nasser replaced King Farouk as leader of Egypt.

Sadat held many government positions under Nasser. He remained loyal and hardworking and Nasser rewarded him by appointing him vice president. Nasser died of a heart attack and Sadat became President of Egypt.

As President, Sadat worked to give the people of Egypt what they wanted. He cut back the power of the hated secret police, got rid of military experts from the Soviet Union, and improved economic conditions. He ran Egypt single-handedly and tried to modernize the country. He also prepared for war against Israel. In 1973 Sadat made the decision to go to war. On October 6, Egyptian tanks surged across the Suez canal and attacked Israel. The Israelis, with help from the United States, made a

Name____________________________

Date ____________________________

surprisingly strong showing. They pushed back Egyptian and other Arab troops and Sadat realized that the war could not be won. He began peace negotiations that finally resulted in the peace treaty of 1978.

Many people were excited about the promise of peace and admired Sadat's courage to stand alone for what he believed. Others wanted him out of office. They felt he had betrayed the Arab nations. In an act of hatred and violence, some of the soldiers he had often addressed as "my sons" shot and killed him in 1988, ending his mission to bring peace to the Middle East.

Student Activity
International Biographies
Book 1
Lesson 12, Handout 36
Sample

Name________________________

Date ________________________

Anwar Sadat's Decision

Problem: Egypt and other Arab nations are involved in a war with Israel. Sadat believes that the Arabs cannot win the war.

Possible Solution: Sign a peace treaty with Israel

Pros

1. Peace
2. Egypt would not lose men and supplies fighting the war.
3. Money could be used to improve living conditions at home

Cons

1. Israel remains in control of disputed territory.
2. The other Arab nations will become enemies of Egypt.

Decision

Sign peace treaty

Name________________________

Date ________________________

Decisions, Decisions . . .

Scenario 1: You have friends that want you to try drugs. You must make a choice.

Scenario 2: Your friends have tried alcohol and want you to be one of the gang. You don't want to drink.

Scenario 3: A new student comes to your school. Your friends don't think this person is "cool" enough to be a part of your group. Make a stand by being a friend to the new student.

Scenario 4: In your neighborhood all of your friends are in a gang. They want you to join, too, but you don't want to. You have to choose between what you want to do and what they want you to do.

Scenario 5: Someone wants to cheat from you on a test, homework, or an answer in class. What do you do? *or* You see someone cheating on a test. Do you tell the teacher or do you confront the person? Do you just keep it to yourself?

Name________________________

Date ________________________

My Decision

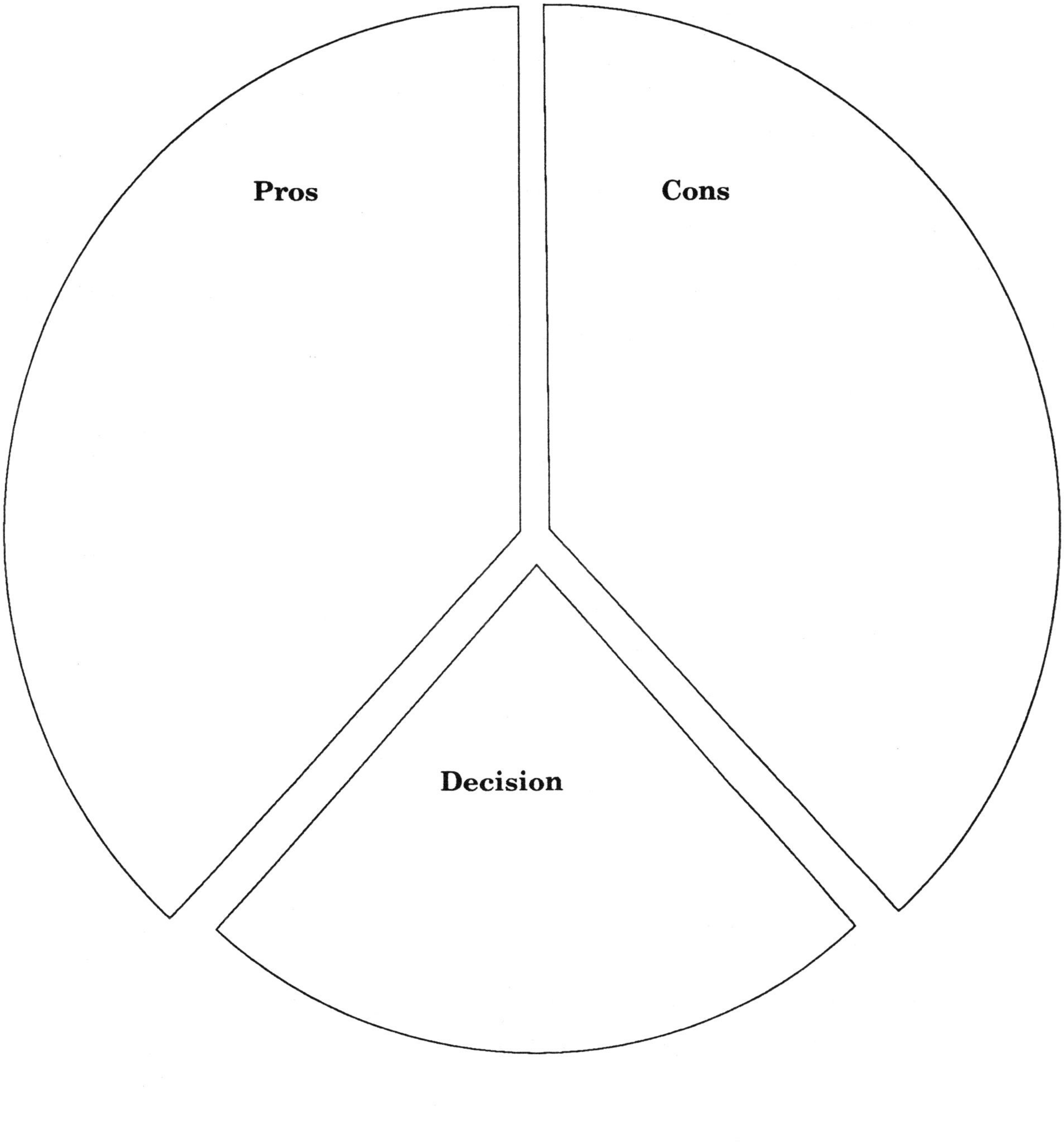

Haile Selassie

Objectives

- To identify Haile Salassie as Ethiopia's last emperor
- To create a commemorative symbol of Selassie's rule

Notes to the Teacher

This lesson involves the country of Ethiopia. It would be helpful to gather some current information about the country as it is today. Pictures of the country can be found in the library in books about nations. The problem of famine within this country is often in the news and efforts made by groups around the world to alleviate their hunger problems could also be discussed. It is also appropriate to examine the geography of Ethiopia to help explain one of the reasons it was able to remain independent over the centuries.

Students read a biography of Selassie and discuss his strength and leadership in bringing Ethiopia into the modern age. They continue to explore his character by designing a traditional obelisk using symbols and words that depict him as the "Lion of Judah" and a leader of his people.

INTERDISCIPLINARY STRANDS:
Art, English/Language Arts, Geography, History, Political Science

MATERIALS:
Handouts 39,40, and 41 paper or white cloth (felt or muslin), colored felt pieces or other fabric, scissors, crayons or markers, world wall map

TERMS:
catechism, constitution, Coptic Christians, enlargement, emperor, heir, League of Nations, curved and straight lines, obelisk, regent, ritual, thumbnail sketch, wattle

Resources

Abebe, Daniel. *Ethiopia in Pictures.* Minneapolis: Lerner Publications, Co. 1988.
Mosley, Leonard. *Haile Selassie: The Conquering Lion.* Englewood Cliffs, New Jersey: Prentice-Hall, Inc., 1964.
Negash, Askale. *Haile Selassie.* New York: Chelsea House Publishers, 1989.
Schwab, Peter, ed. *Ethiopia & Haile Selassie.* New York: Facts on File, Inc., 1972.

Procedure

1. Ask students to fold a sheet of paper in half and on one side write what they would like to do when they are adults. On the other side, ask them to write what their parents expect them to do. Share their answers and discuss.

2. Ask students if they are in agreement with their parents' wishes. Why/why not? Explain that in the past, parents often decided the future of their children: their jobs, their mates, etc. Tell them that they will be reading about a man whose father wanted him to be the emperor of his country and that he wanted the same thing.

3. Locate Ethiopia on a world wall map. Discuss its geography of mountainous plateaus cut by deep river valleys with desert-like land surrounding the plateaus. Note the city of Addeis Ababa and the fact that Ethiopia is an ancient country, dating back to 1000 B.C. Ethiopia comes from the Greek word for "burnt face" because of the dark-skinned people who lived there.

4. Discuss the biography using the following questions:
   a. Why did Haile Selassie get the nickname, the Lion of Judah?
      Did what they read about him indicate strength and leadership? Do lions share some of the same traits as Selassie did?
   b. Do they feel that his road to power was an easy one?
   c. What was the constitution like? Was it like ours? Why was it different? Could it have been like ours? Why not?
   d. Compare Ethiopia before and after Selassie's rule. How was it changed?

5. Distribute **Handout 40** and ask students to create a commemorative obelisk in the fashion of the ancient Ethiopians. What words and symbols might they place on their obelisk? Brainstorm some ideas as a group before they start their individual work.

6. Distribute **Handout 41**. Have students create *their own* stylized lion banners by using the handout for their thumbnail sketch lion designs.Stress the use of stylized curve lines and straight lines as shown on the sample lion. Once a thumbnail sketch is decided upon, have students enlarge their designs onto a piece of yellow, red, or some other color of felt or other fabric. Cut a piece of fabric rectangle just a bit larger than the lion and then glue or sew the lion to the white background fabric so that the lion fills the fabric close to the edges of the banner.

7. Display their completed obelisks and banners.

Enrichment/Extension

1. Research and make a map of Ethiopia as it is today showing physical features, manufactured products, agricultural products, population, etc. (See Appendix, **Handout 45**.)

2. Research to find out more about the famines in Ethiopia and the reasons for them. Determine the government's role in the problem—are they a help or a hindrance? What have other countries done to assist Ethiopia?
   Then: Create posters about Ethiopia and the need for food and other help. Funds could be collected to donate to the world funds that aid hunger at home and abroad.

3. Research the hunger and the homeless problems at home. Make posters and collect money to support help programs within your own community.

4. Other potential lessons relating to the problems facing Africa can be found in "Identifying Problems in Which Decisions Are Required," *World Cultures / World History* (Villa Maria, Pa.: The Center for Learning, 1988).

Art Notation

Haile Selassie's portrait depicts him in his prime as the leader of Ethiopia. The square in which the portrait is placed represents Ethiopia and the circle in the background represents his role as Ethiopia's spokesperson to the world. (See Appendix, **Handout 58**.)

Name________________________

Date ________________________

Haile Selassie

In a round mud and wattle hut in Ethiopia on July 23, 1892, something very exciting was happening. Today Ras Makonnen would get the son that he wanted so badly. His wife, Waizero Yeshimabeit, and her servants had been at the hut since May because the city was so hot and dangerous with diseases. Out in the countryside, they enjoyed the healthy air and the Ras (duke) could continue the business of managing his province of Harar, Ethiopia. They were hoping for a healthy baby this time. She had already had eight babies that had not lived.

Name______________________

Date ______________________

As the baby boy was born, a terrific thunderstorm began with heavy rain and lightning. This was a good sign because Ethiopia always needed rain! The women lifted their voices in praise, and the midwife rubbed the ritual butter on the baby's lips. All the rifles in the village were fired and the Ras's soldiers fell to their knees in prayer. Cattle were killed for a celebration feast that would last for two days.

When little Tafari was a month old, the family traveled back to their home in Harar so that he could be baptized in the Coptic Church there. Ethiopia was a mixture of people: some Muslim, some Christians, some Jewish, and some who held other beliefs. The Coptic Christians were the ruling group in Ethiopia. No one realized that they were celebrating the birth of a future Emperor of Ethiopia when they heard his baptismal name, Haile Selassie!

Tafari's father, the Ras Makonnen, was a good friend of Ethiopia's Emperor Menelik. The Emperor trusted Ras Makonnen in political matters because he had been a loyal soldier as well as a friend. It was expected that the Ras would someday be emperor, and the Ras was anxious to have a son to succeed him.

There were no schools in Ethiopia, so his priest taught Tafari his catechism and the Amharic alphabet (his tribal alphabet). When he was ten, his father was sent to London to represent Ethiopia. His father realized how valuable education was and when he returned hired a French doctor in the village to teach Tafari French. He also learned many other things—one was that his country needed to modernize. There were no schools, no roads, no railroads, and no hospitals. He knew in his heart that someday he would rule Ethiopia and that he would bring progress to his country.

Tafari had an enemy from the time of his birth. A great war lord named Ras Mikael was married to Emperor Menelik's daughter and he had a son, Yasu, who he wanted to be the next emperor. The young boys did not even know each other, and they were already in the middle of a struggle for the throne.

In Ethiopia a son did not always inherit land and titles, a father had to name an heir. That is why Menelik wanted Tafari's father to follow him, but when Tafari was fourteen, his father died. (His mother had died when he was two giving birth to her ninth child.) Tafari had to leave Harar and live in another province because Menelik felt he was too young to rule

Name________________________

Date ________________________

Harar alone. His half-brother was given that job. Tafari stayed for awhile in the emperor's court and attended a new school in Addis Ababa started by Menelik. He studied languages, economics, history, and religion.

In school Tafari planned for the things he wanted to correct someday. He wanted to end slavery. He hated the slave markets. He wanted to make paved roads, to have electric lights for everyone, and to start schools.

When Menelik had several strokes, his wife, an ambitious woman, ran the affairs of Ethiopia. She wanted her son, Yasu, to succeed Menelik, and eventually he got the job instead of Tafari, but Yasu was too interested in drinking and having a good time to take an interest in Ethiopia. Many people were upset but could do nothing. Finally, they got Menelik's daughter to become the empress with Tafari acting as her regent and king. Manelik's daughter was just a figure-head. Tafari really ran the country.

Tafari, or Haile Selassie as he became known, wanted to change Ethiopia into a modern nation, but many people tried to stop him. The church did not want to modernize because it meant educating the people. They were sure it was best to keep them ignorant. The other dukes did not want to lose their power because Haile Selassie wanted them to give up their slaves and to share their wealth with the people. He needed the help of knowlegable people from other countries to make the changes, but Ethiopians did not want foreigners and did not want them in their country. Despite opposition, Selassie began to invite people in to help, and he also had Ethiopia join the League of Nations, hopeful that this would help him find people to assist in modernizing his country as well as keep peace in the world. He began to build schools and roads and other improvements. Attempts were often made by the empress and others to overthrow him as king or to wreck his plans, but he was a patient man and managed to stay in charge.

On April 2, 1930, the Empress Zauditu died. After forty days of mourning and the rainy season had passed, Haile Selassie was anointed emperor with holy oils by the Coptic Archbishop Kyril, on November 2, 1930. Now he really began his efforts toward progress, including the granting of a constitution to give the people more say in their government. Because Ethiopians were not ready for complete democracy, the constitution was more of a practice document. Emperor Selassie believed that the population must be educated in order for democracy to work and to last.

Name________________________

Date ________________________

All progress came to a stop in 1935 when the Italian army under Benito Mussolini marched into Ethiopia. Mussolini fought the Ethiopians with modern weapons, tanks, and planes while they had only spears, old rifles, and an airforce of six airplanes. The Ethiopian army wore uniforms with Ethiopian colors, but they refused to wear shoes. They were no match for the whole Italian Army.

Haile Selassie fought with his men on the front lines but was at last persuaded to go with his family to London until he could be restored to power. He spoke to the League of Nations asking for help against Mussolini and warned them that other countries would be next, but the League would not listen. The war eventually developed into World War II and all of Europe became involved.

After World War II Emperor Selassie returned to rebuild his country. Several countries sent aid and President Franklin D. Roosevelt of the United States promised help. Money, machines, and people with experience came to Ethiopia to build, roads, schools, and hospitals. The constitution was revised and the people got the right to vote. Even though he believed in peace, Selassie built a small army trained by Swedes, British, and Americans. In fact, he even sent some troops to help the United Nations in 1952, during the Korean Conflict.

On September 12, 1974, Haile Selassie I was removed from office. He was old and people backed by the Soviet Union wanted power. He was held prisoner in the old Menelik palace and never seen in public again. Selassie died on August 28, 1975, from circulatory failure. He had taken Ethiopia into the modern world. Most of his dreams for his country had come true. He was the last emperor of Ethiopia and truly the Lion of Judah!

Name____________________

Date ____________________

Creating a Commemorative Obelisk

In ancient Ethiopia, in the kingdom of Aksum, giant pillars or obelisks were set up. On the pillars were symbols and phrases that served to honor an important person. Think of phrases and symbols that would tell about Haile Selassie if such a pillar were made for him.

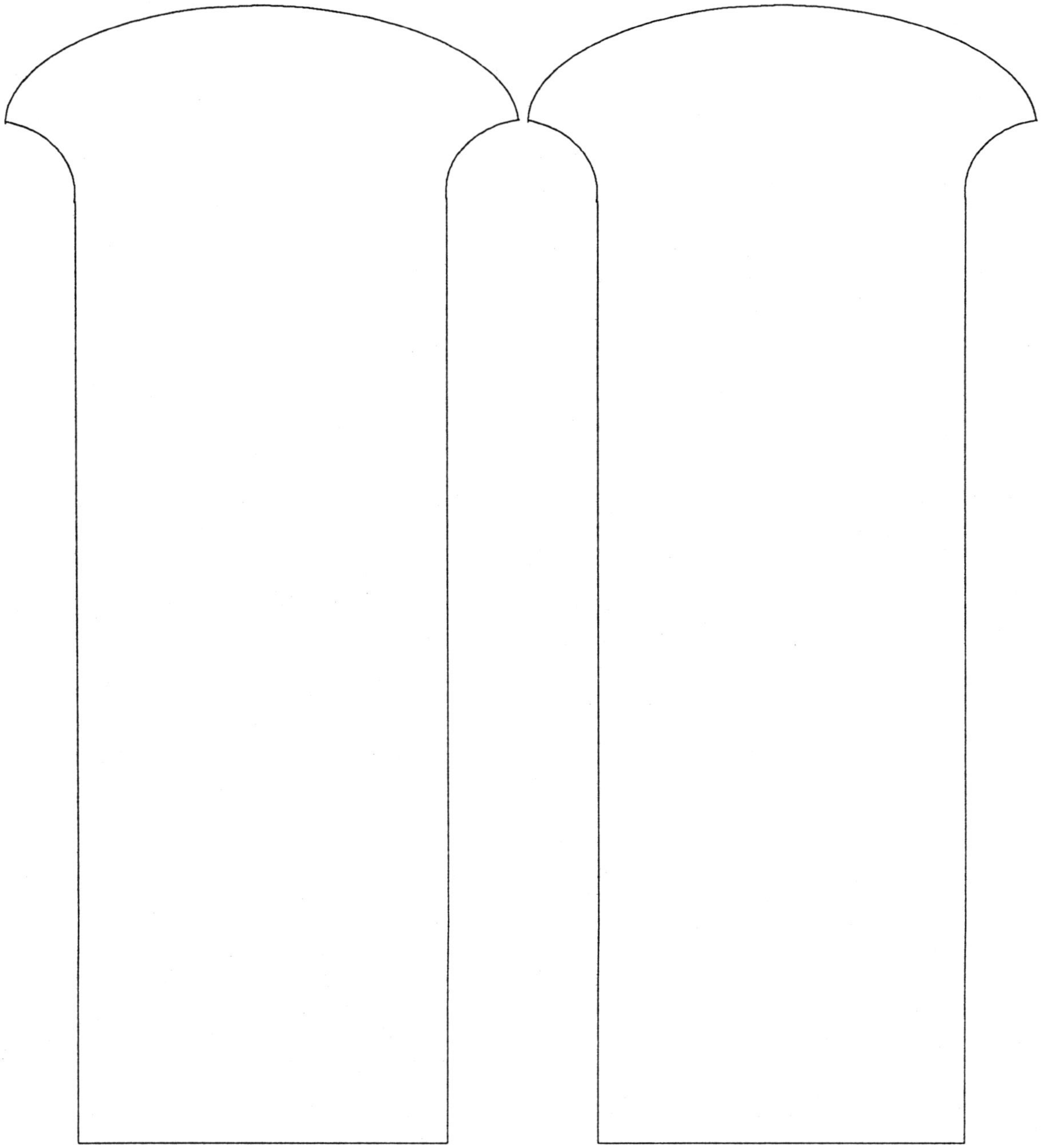

Name________________________

Date ________________________

Creating a Banner

In the large markets of Ethiopia, you can find many wonderful rugs and tapestries made of cloth woven by the people. They are colorful and have creative designs. Look at the sample stylized lion and use the space below to create a thumbnail sketch stylized lion to be used in your design for a banner that might be made in Ethiopia in honor of Haile Selassie, the Lion of Judah.

Shaka Zulu

Objectives

- To identify the contributions of Shaka Zulu as an African tribal chief
- To make a comic strip depicting an event in Shaka's life

Notes to the Teacher

The Zulu were a relatively unknown African tribe until the early 1800s when Shaka became chief. Through new military techniques, complete control of his warriors, and instilling fear in neighboring tribes, Shaka conquered a wide area of what is now South Africa and built his tribe into a powerful unit. In 1828 he was assassinated by two of his brothers. Without the firm control of Shaka, the Zulu gradually lost power and were finally defeated by the British at Ulundi in 1879. The Zulu name now applies to over two and a half million Bantu-speaking people who live in specially reserved tribal homelands in the Natal and Transvaal provinces of South Africa.

INTERDISCIPLINARY STRANDS:
Art, English/Language Arts, Geography, History, Political Science

MATERIALS:
Handouts 42, 43, and 44 paper, crayons or markers, world wall map

TERMS:
clan, cunning, ethnic, flank, illegitimate, kraal, regiment, ridicule, Zulu

Resources

Jefferson, Margo and Skinner, Eliot. *Roots of Time.* New York: Doubleday & Co., 1974.
Keating, Bern. *Shaka: King of the Zulus.* New York: G.P. Putnam's Sons, 1968.
Murphy, E. Jefferson. *Understanding Africa.* New York: Thomas Y. Crowell, 1979.
Musgrove, Margaret. *Ashanti to Zulu, African Traditions.* New York: Franklin Watts Inc., 1967.
Neurath, Marie. *They Lived Like This in Africa.* New York: Franklin Watts Inc., 1967.
Stamley, Diane and Venneman, Peter. *Shaka: King of the Zulus.* New York: Morrow Junior Books, 1988.

Procedure

1. Ask students if they have ever heard of Shaka Zulu. Discuss what they have read or seen in the movies. Make note of the stereotyping of African natives by Hollywood.

2. Locate South Africa and the Tugela River on a world wall map and explain that this is where the Zulu tribe lived.

3. Read **Handout 42** and discuss the life of Shaka Zulu. Emphasize his importance to the Zulus. Help students discuss how he differed from the Hollywood stereotype.

4. Explain the depiction of a story in comic strip format. Use **Handout 43** as an example. Stress that this is an exercise to see if they can present important information in a logical, visual format. Point out the factual details such as the cow horn formation and the success of the Zulu troops.

5. Distribute **Handout 44** and have students design their own comic strip of Shaka Zulu. Have reference books that depict African clothing, etc. available for class use.

6. Display the finished comic strips. Have students share them with a lower grade.

Enrichment/Extension

1. Investigate a tribe of Africa, and present a brief report to the class on the characteristics of the tribe and its contribution to African culture. (See Appendix, **Handout 45**.)

2. Prepare a script depicting the life of Shaka Zulu. Assign parts, practice, and perform the play for a lower grade.

3. Transfer the student-made comic strips onto film. Use strips of acetate that will fit into a filmstrip projector. Use permanent fine-tip markers to draw the comics onto the acetate. View the finished filmstrips by running the acetate through the filmstrip projector.

4. Other potential lessons relating to the tribes of Africa can be found in: "Tribal Organization in Africa," and "African Culture—Zulu War/British vs. Zulu," *World History, Books 2* and *3* (Villa Maria, Pa.: The Center for Learning, 1986).

Art Notation

Shaka Zulu's portrait depicts him as a young warrior in Zulu tribal clothing and fashion. A Zulu warrior's shield is shown within the circle in the background (See Appendix, **Handout 58.**)

Name____________________

Date ____________________

Shaka Zulu

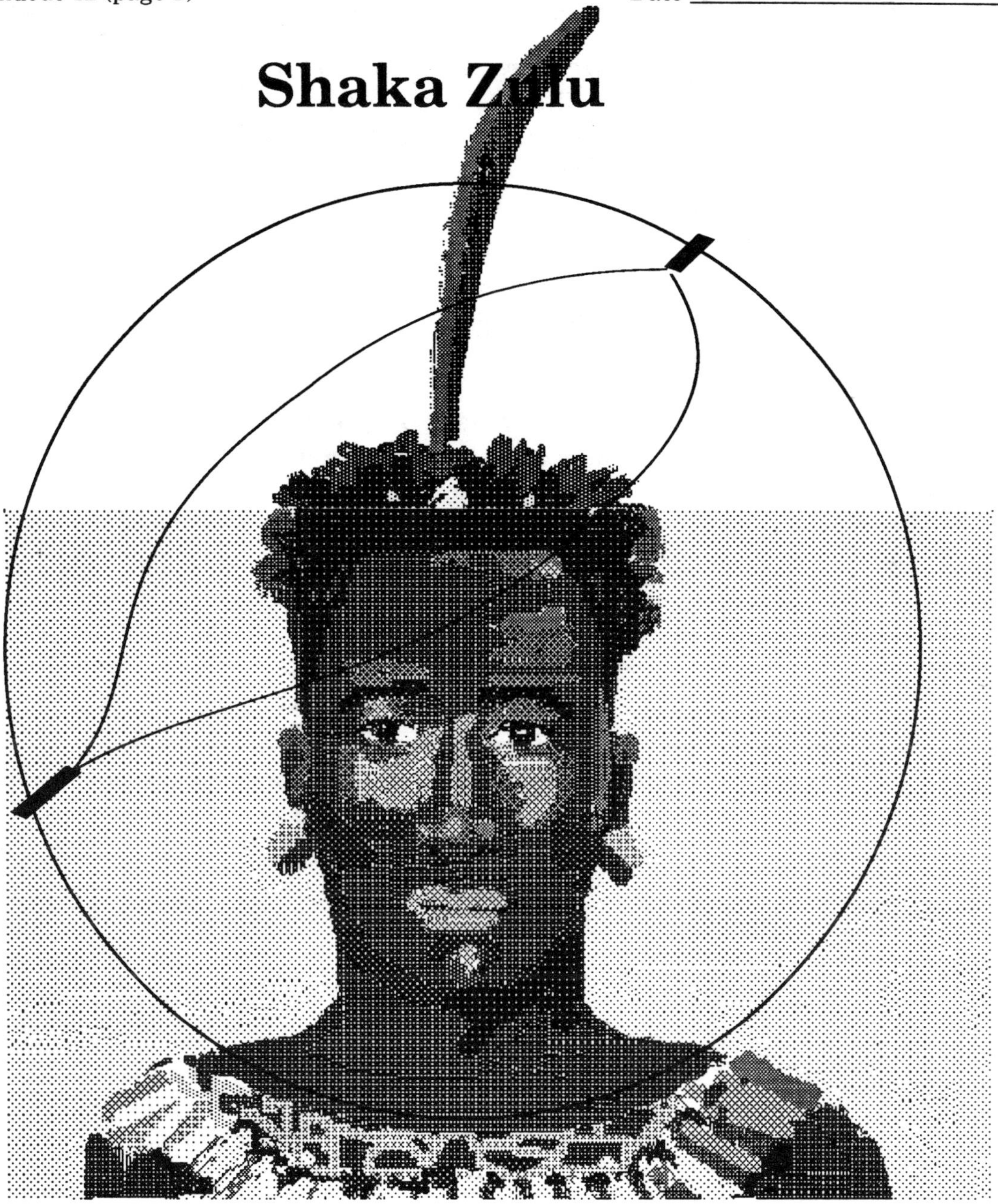
*

Once upon a time in a land far away, a baby boy was born. His father rejected him. He was loved by his mother, but she was poor and could give him little beyond words of encouragement. Other children made fun of him. Even his name, given to him by his uncle, meant "the Beetle" and was an insult. This same baby boy grew up to be the greatest chief of his tribe!

*This is an artist's rendition based on a drawing made from photographs of Shaka Zulu's closest relatives.

Name________________________

Date ________________________

This potential fairy tale is a true story. The time was 1787 in a place now known as the Republic of South Africa. The chief who rejected his son was Senzagakona. The mother who loved and encouraged him was Nandi. The poor, mocked baby boy became Shaka, the all-powerful chief of the Zulus!

Senzagakona and Nandi could not marry because they were of the same clan so Shaka grew up as an illegitimate son. He was teased and treated as an outcast by his tribe. This difficult childhood may account for the strength and determination he developed as a young man. It may also account for the streak of cruelty he displayed at various times as an adult. Shaka's mother was the only one who believed in him, and she encouraged him to be strong and overcome the ridicule of others.

Shaka had both brawn and brain. He was brave in battle and fought tirelessly. He also improved the spear, the traditional weapon of the Zulus, and made it possible to change the way their armies did battle.

The usual battle plan, which was used by both the Zulus and their enemies, was to run toward the enemy throwing their spears as they ran. They would then pick up spears that had been thrown at them and use them in similar fashion. Shaka shortened the spear and used it like a sword. It was a much more effective way to fight because the spear remained in the warrior's hand and could be used again and again at close range to kill the enemy.

A successful warrior, Shaka was made chief when he was only thirty years old. He devised a new battle plan. Instead of lining up and rushing at the enemy, Shaka put his men in a new formation, called the cow's horns. The main part of the army stayed in the middle and two regiments branched out—one on each side like the horns of a cow—to encircle the enemy and destroy him from the sides (flanks) and behind. It worked very well.

Shaka organized his army and trained them carefully. They were housed in separate kraals, or villages, by regiments. They had to get permission from Shaka to marry. He forced his men to give up their oxhide sandals, toughen the soles of their feet, and fight barefooted. They were trained for endurance; they could run barefooted fifty miles per day over the rough African countryside, a feat no other army has ever been able to match.

Name______________________

Date ______________________

Shaka's army was taught to run in unison and to wait quietly for battle commands. Before, they had run screaming and yelling at their enemies in a haphazard fashion. Now, on command, the warriors would stamp their feet and hit their oxhide shields in unison. This was an awesome scene for the tribes who were not used to seeing such a controlled display of power. The Zulus became experts at using their new short spears and carrying out orders. They soon gained a reputation as fierce warriors, led by the cunning Shaka. Before long, Shaka had captured many tribes, increasing his army and training new warriors all the time. Eventually, his army numbered over 40,000.

Things went well for Shaka until his mother died. Throughout his life his mother had always stood by him. She encouraged him and told him he would triumph in the end. He loved her very much, and his grief at her death was great. He ordered all Zulus to mourn for a year and established strict rules. After the cows were milked, the milk was to be poured on the ground—no one was to drink milk. No one was to plant, cultivate, or harvest crops. The people faced starvation until Shaka relented and relaxed the mourning rules a few months later.

Shaka started to have trouble with what had been the key to his success—the army. It was so big now that he could not command it personally but had to rely on others. The Zulus had conquered so much territory that many regiments were far away from their home kraals for long periods of time. Saddened by his mother's death, Shaka gave full reign to his streak of cruelty. Resentment against him grew.

His half-brothers, who had long been jealous of Shaka, saw their chance to take over. Their plot to kill Shaka was successful and his half-brother, Dingane, became king. Other chiefs followed Dingane and the Zulus were eventually defeated by the British about fifty years later.

Shaka was gone but not forgotten. In the twelve years he had been king, he had transformed the little Zulu tribe into a mighty nation. Today, the Zulus are the major ethnic group of South Africa. Shaka's name and heroic deeds are passed on by the Zulus generation to generation. The poor, outcast Zulu boy is recorded in world history as a military genius and compared with Napoleon and Alexander the Great.[1]

[1]Adapted from: *Shaka, King of the Zulus* by Diana Stanley and Peter Venneman (New York: Morrow Junior Books, 1988) and *Understanding Africa* by Jefferson Murphy (New York: Thomas Crowell Publishers, 1978).

Student Activity
International Biographies
Book 1
Lesson 14, Handout 43
Sample

Name________________________

Date ________________________

A Comic Strip of Shaka Zulu

Student Activity
International Biographies
Book 1
Lesson 14, Handout 44

Name________________________

Date ________________________

My Comic Strip of Shaka Zulu

Name____________________

Date ____________________

Research Path

11. Make a final draft

10. Proofread

9. Write a first draft

8. Make an outline

7. Cross-reference notecards with bibliography cards

6. Take notes on index cards

5. Make bibliography cards

4. Go to library—check availability of materials

3. Narrow topic

2. Read a textbook and encyclopedia for an overview of topic

1. Select a topic

Student Activity
International Biographies
Book 1
Appendix, Handout 46

Name______________________

Date ______________________

I Read . . .

It was written by . . .

It was published in . . .

It was published by . . .

The latest copyright is . . .

The length of the book is . . .

Name________________________

Date ________________________

You were there...
Tell us all about it...

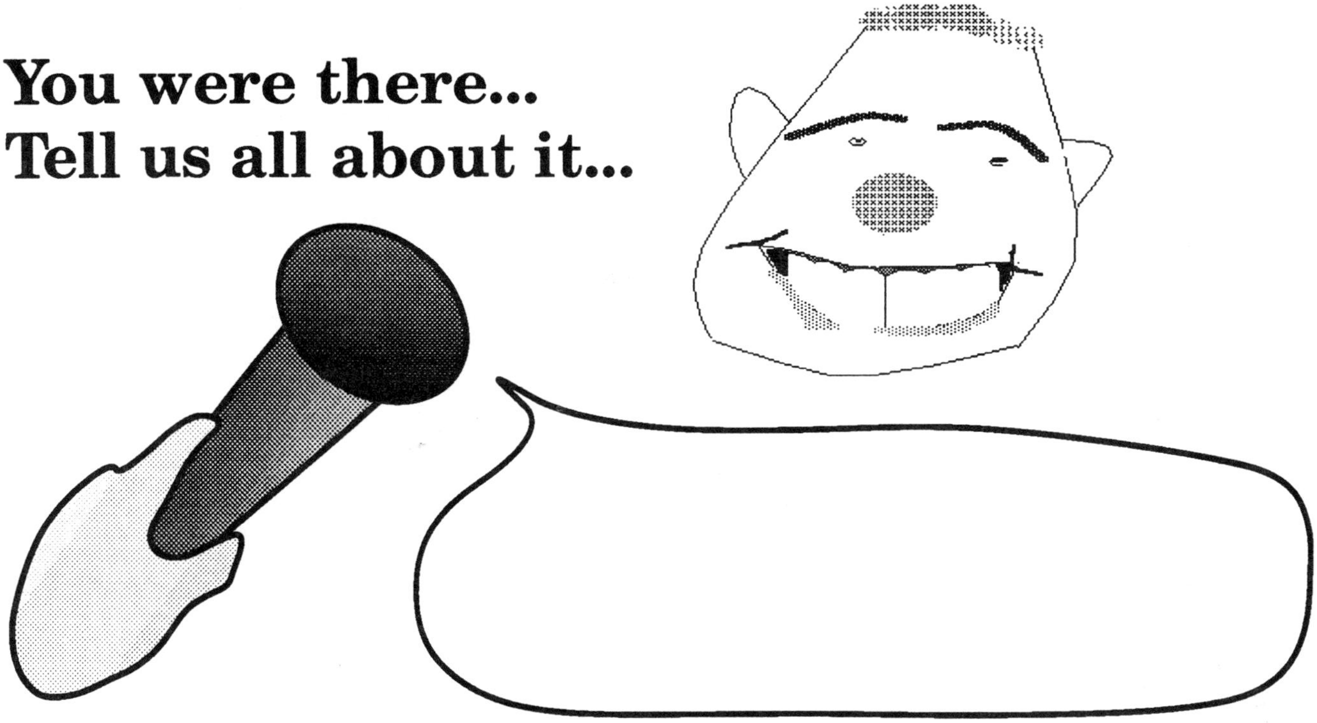

*List below 5 questions you want to ask about your topic:

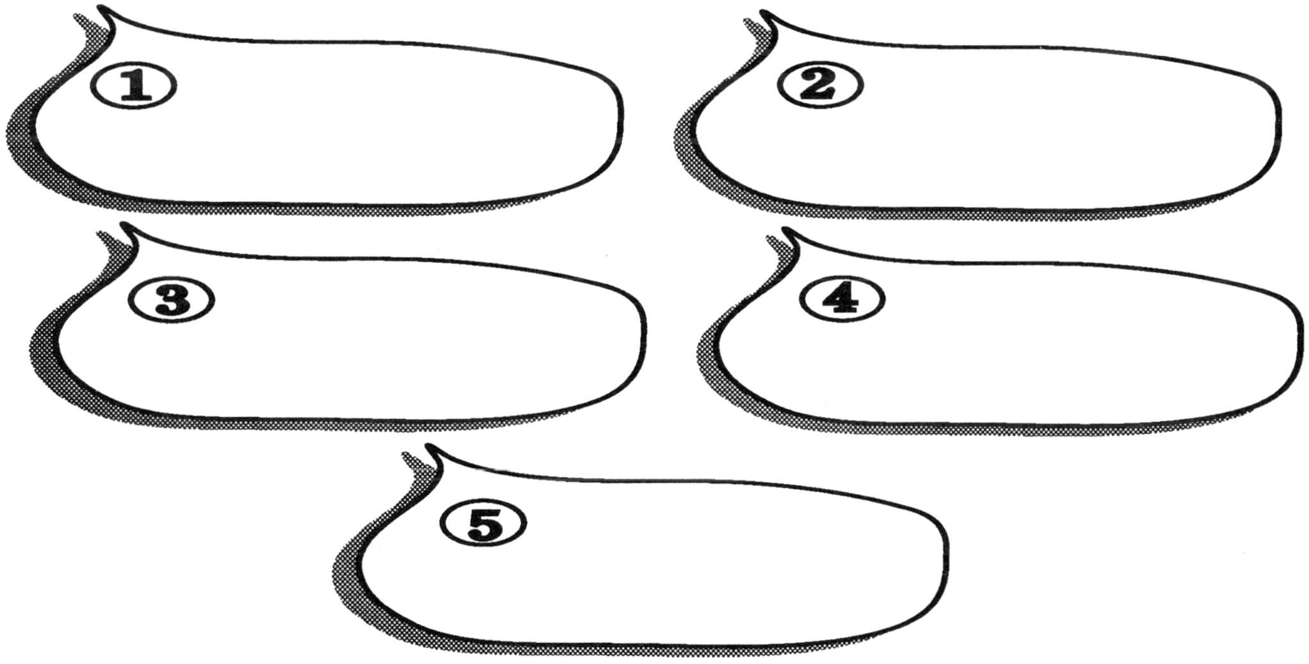

*Write the responses on a separate sheet of paper.

Name______________________

Date ______________________

Our Gang

Leader
Keeps the group going. Helps them stay on task. Sees to it that everyone has a fair say in group's decisions.

Recorder
Keeps the records for the group and makes a neatly written copy if one is needed. Provides everyone in the group a copy if one is needed.

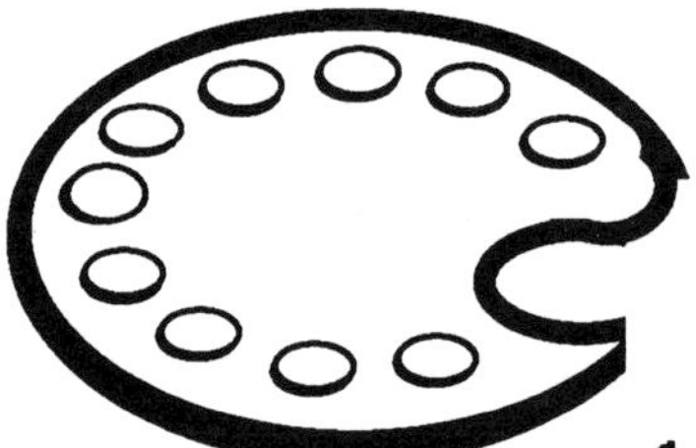

Artist
Does the artwork for the group and/or helps others with their share of the artwork.

Encourager
Sees to it that all take part and that everyone has something to do. Assists the leader in keeping tasks moving along.

Checker
Tracks the group's decisions and makes sure that they are carried out.

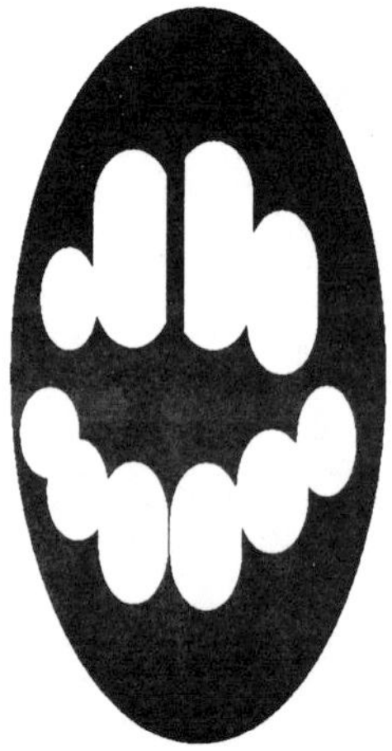

Spokesperson
Any one of the above persons may be selected by the group to give a presentation if one is required.

Student Activity
International Biographies
Book 1
Appendix, Handout 49

Name________________________

Date ________________________

How Our Group Worked

Directions: Make an X on each face that shows how you feel about your work in the group. Use the back of this sheet for additional comments.

	Excellent	Good	Fair	Poor
I was cooperative				
I was polite.				
I did my share.				
I used a quiet voice.				
I helped get materials.				
I helped get ideas.				
I let others do their share.				
I encouraged others.				
I helped organize us.				
I helped us stay on task.				
I helped clean up.				
I did my very best				
My group worked well together.				

Name____________________________

Date ____________________________

How Our Group's Members Worked

Directions: Write a group member's name on a puzzle piece. Then tell what each one contributed to your group that helped the group complete its task.

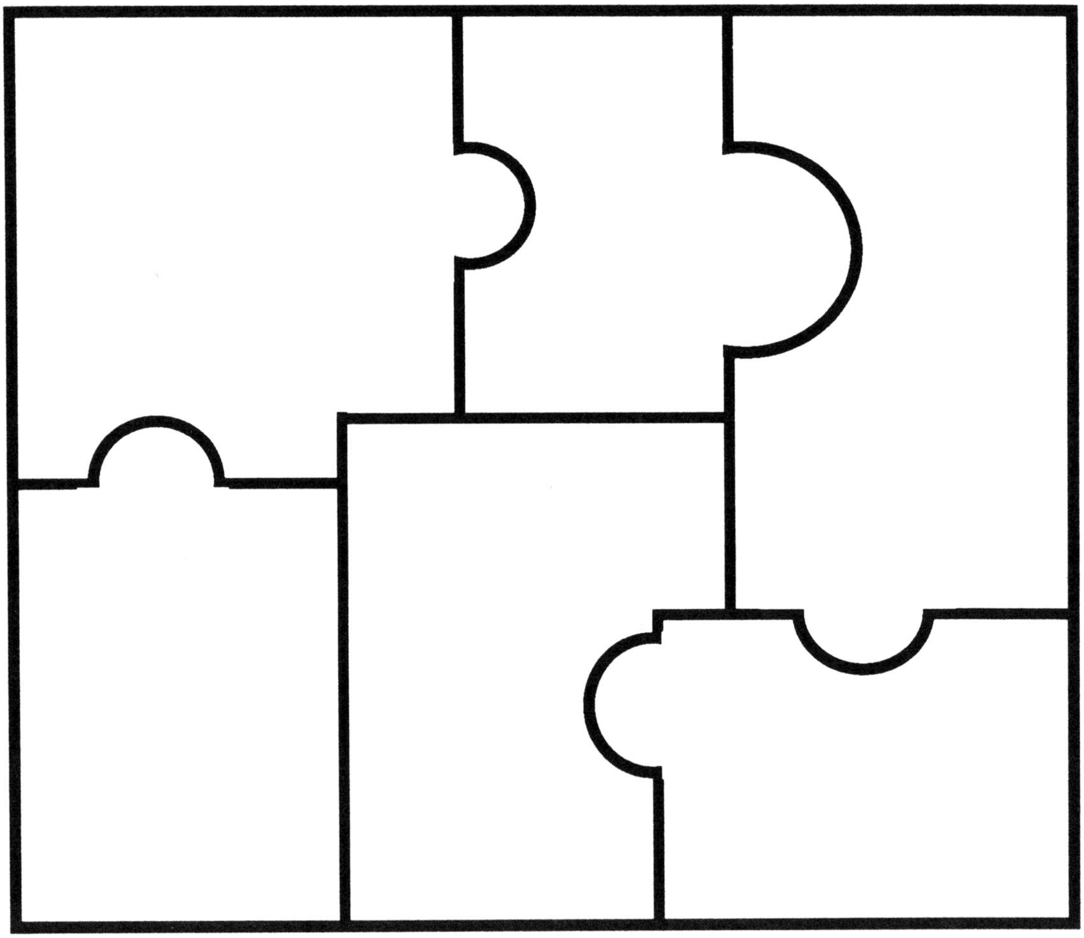

If there was one thing you could change about the way your group worked, what would it be?

____

____

____

Student Activity
International Biographies
Book 1
Appendix, Handout 51

Name________________________

Date ________________________

A Biographical Timeline of ______________________

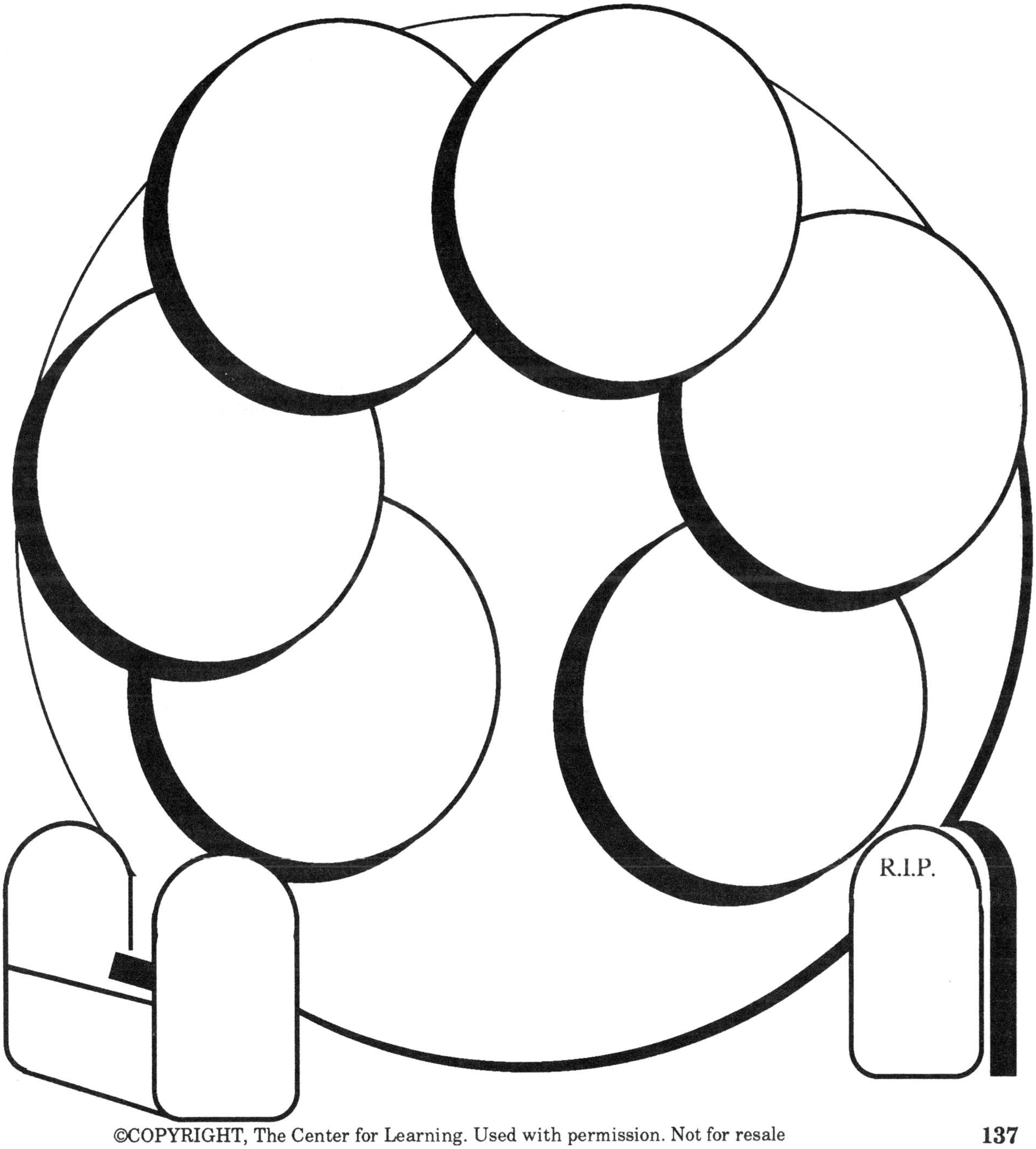

Student Activity
International Biographies
Book 1
Appendix, Handout 52

Name____________________

Date ____________________

Who Is in the News?

Student Activity
International Biographies
Book 1
Appendix, Handout 53

Name________________________

Date ________________________

Making Decisions

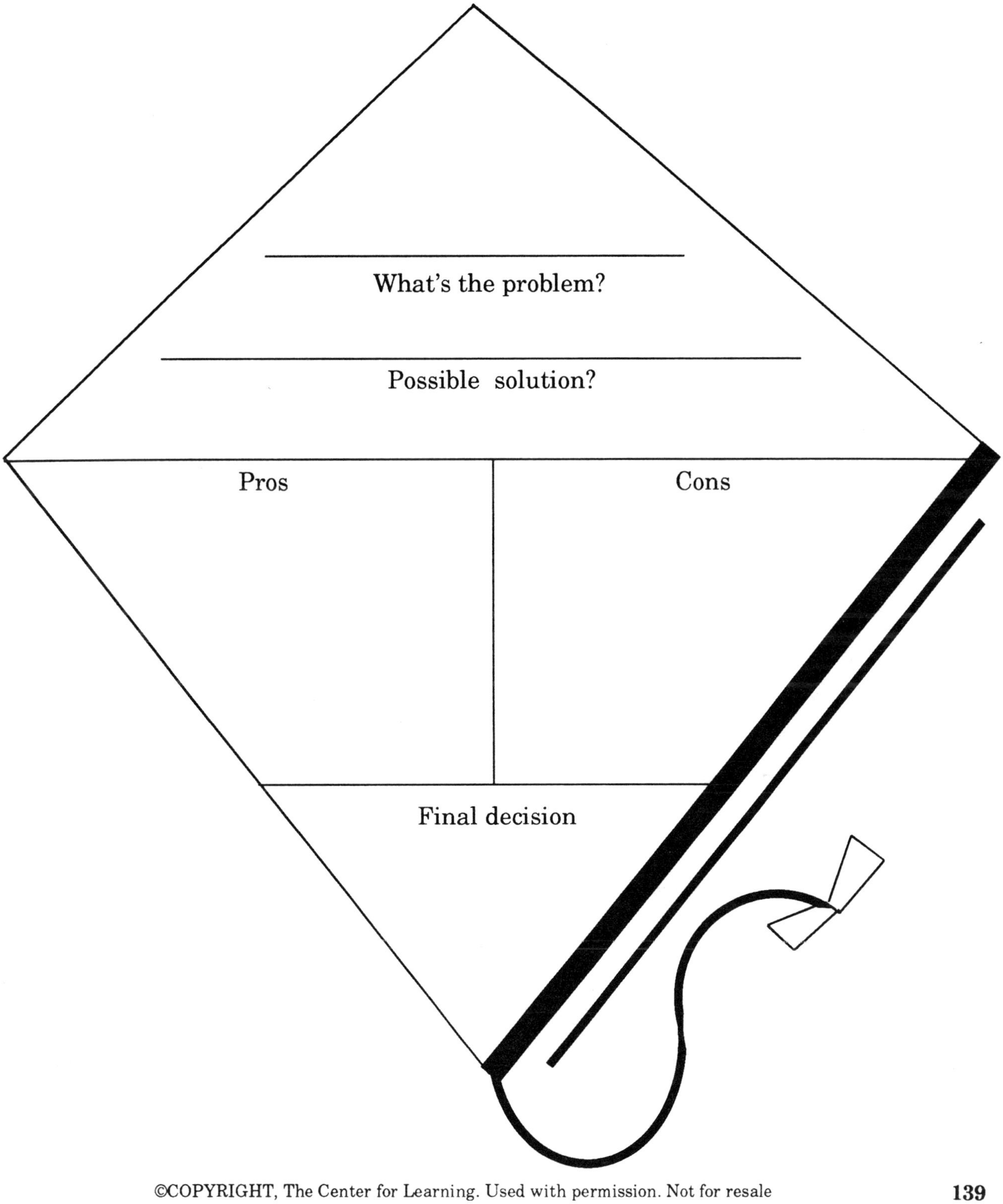

Student Activity
International Biographies
Book 1
Appendix, Handout 54

Name________________________

Date ________________________

The World (Physical)[1]

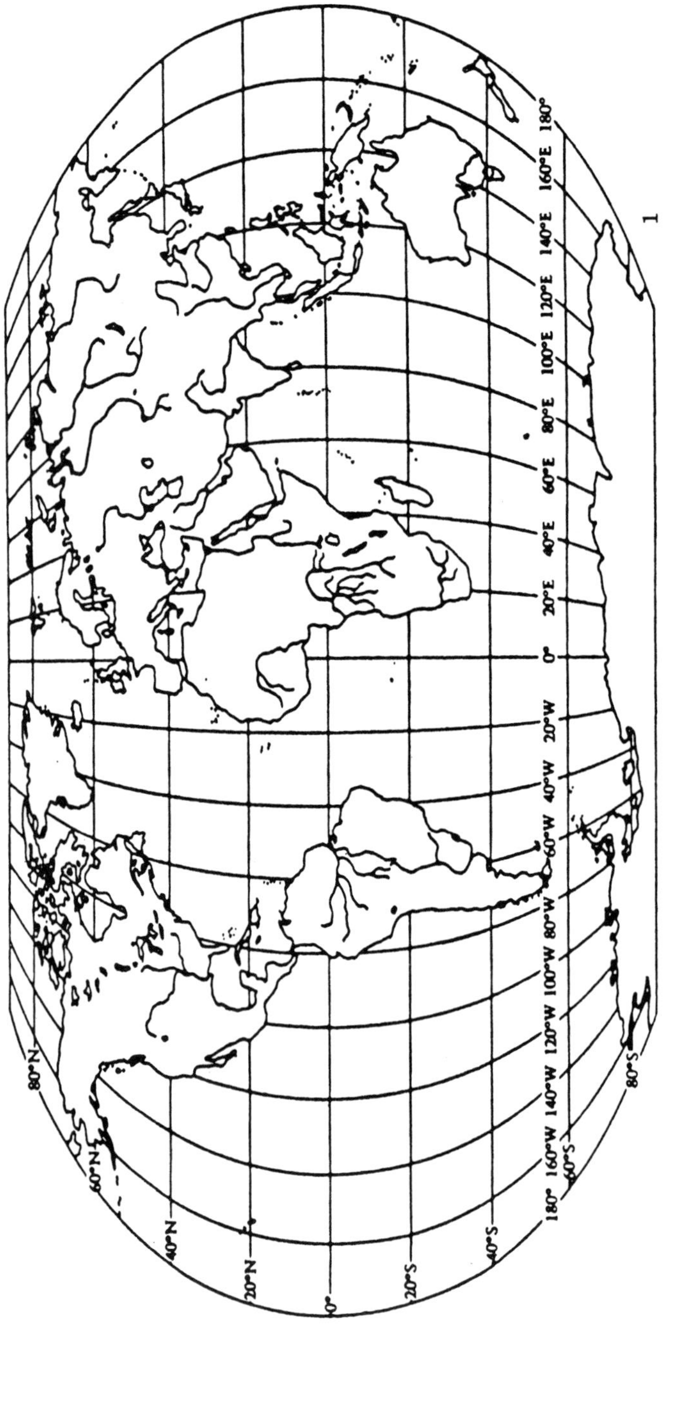

[1]*Maps: An Ancillary Program Support* (Lexington: Mass.: D.C. Heath and Company, 1987).

Student Activity
International Biographies
Book 1
Appendix, Handout 55

Name______________________

Date ______________________

Countries of the World (Political)[2]

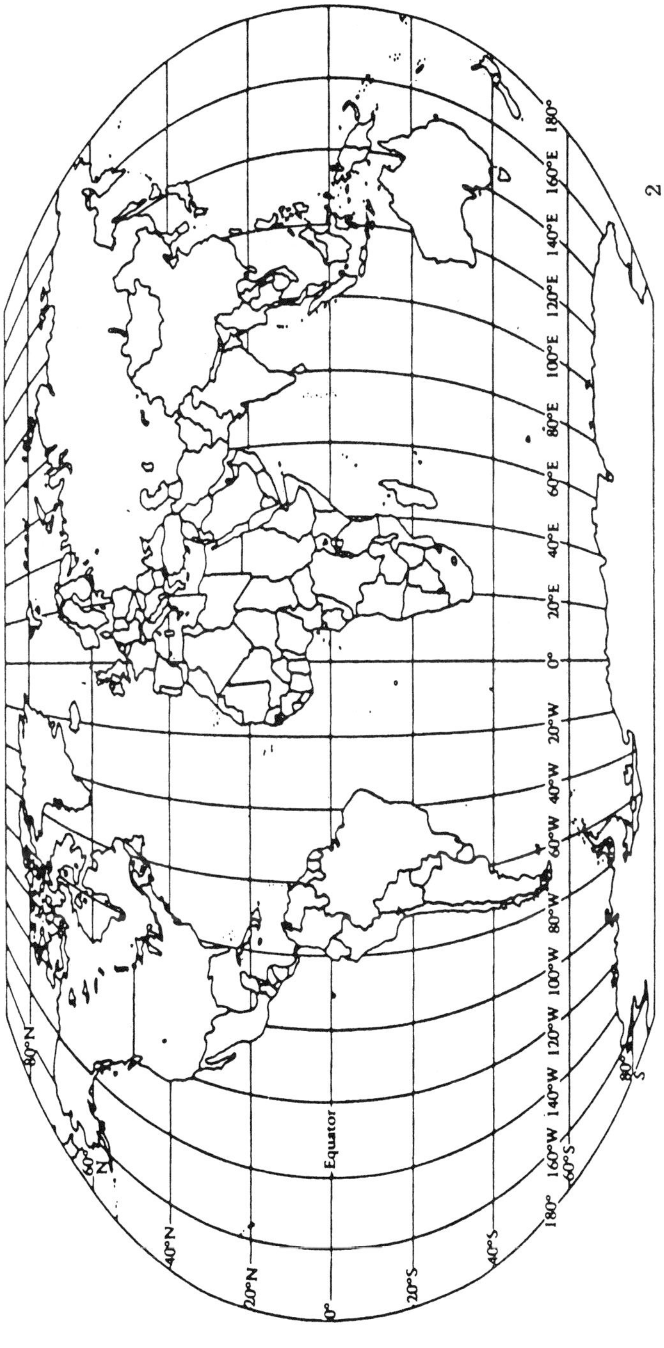

[2]*Maps: An Ancillary Program Support* (Lexington: Mass.: D.C. Heath and Company, 1987).

Student Activity
International Biographies
Book 1
Appendix, Handout 56

Name________________________

Date ________________________

Africa/Middle East (Physical)

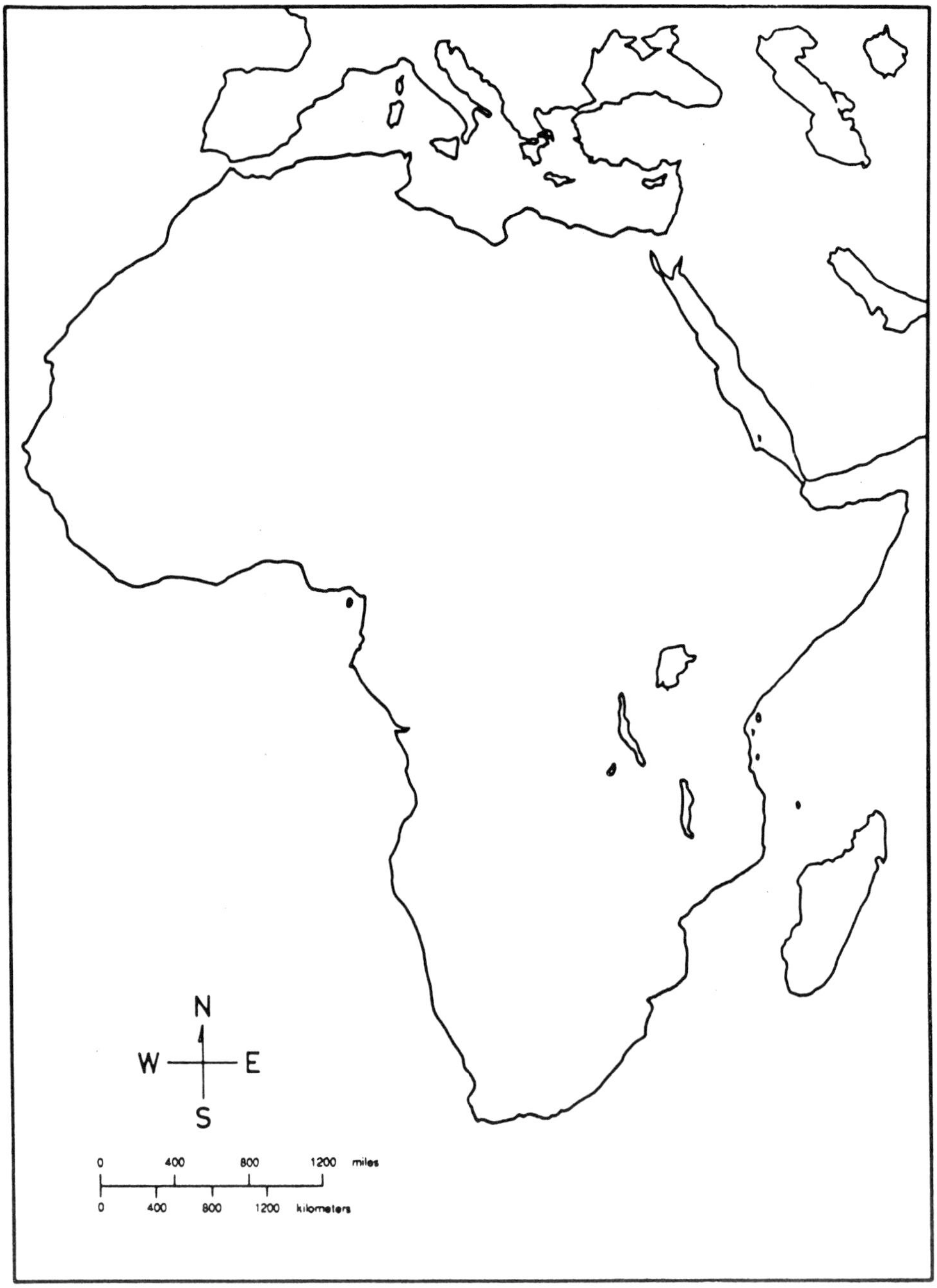

[3]

[3]Adapted from *Merrill Social Studies: Outline Map Resource Book* (Columbus, Ohio: Charles E. Merrill Publishing Company, 1986), 36.

Student Activity
International Biographies
Book 1
Appendix, Handout 57

Name______________________

Date ______________________

Africa/Middle East (Political)

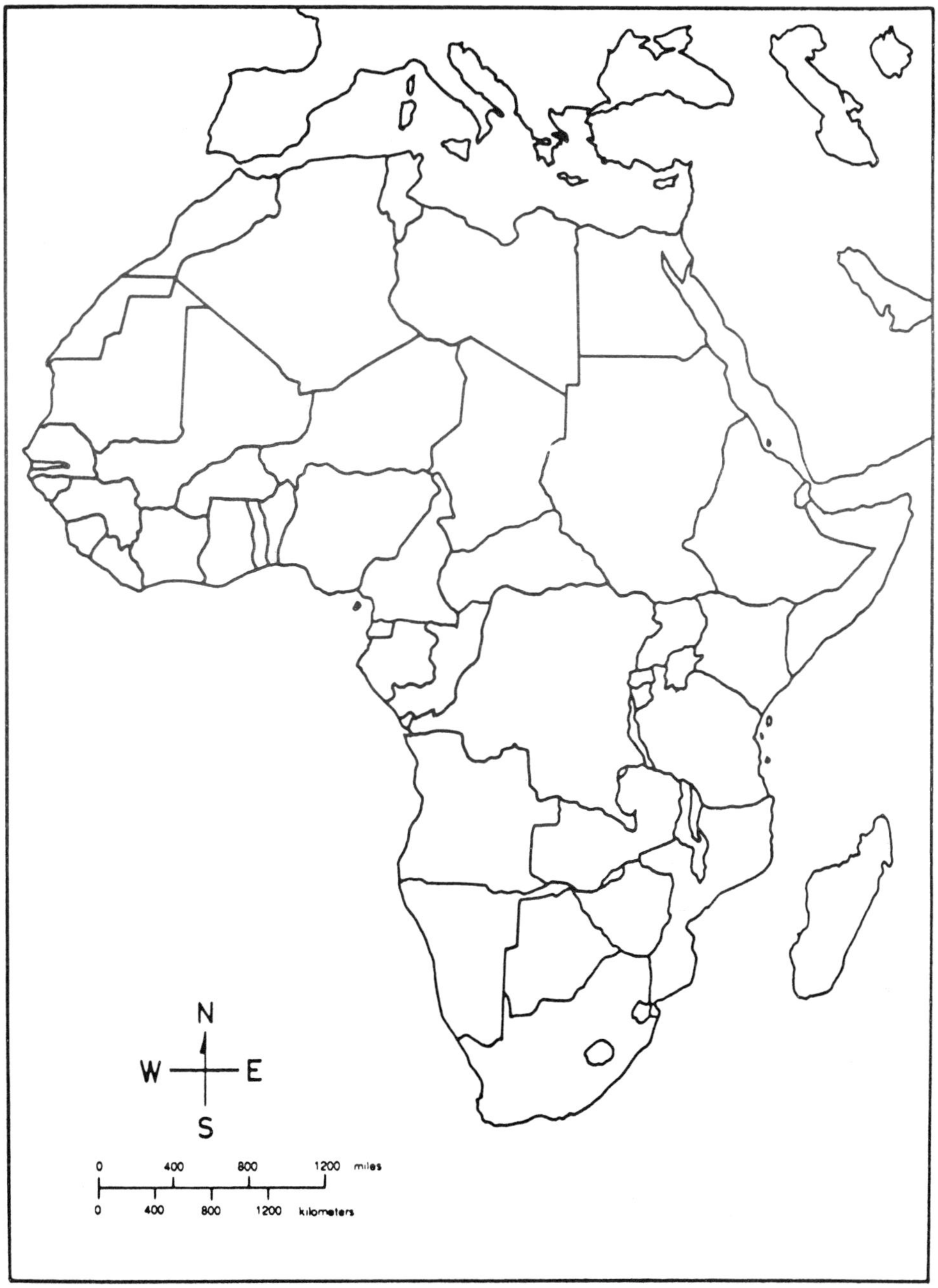

4

[3]Adapted from *Merrill Social Studies: Outline Map Resource Book* (Columbus, Ohio: Charles E. Merrill Publishing Company, 1986), 37.

Name______________________

Date ______________________

Do You See What I See?

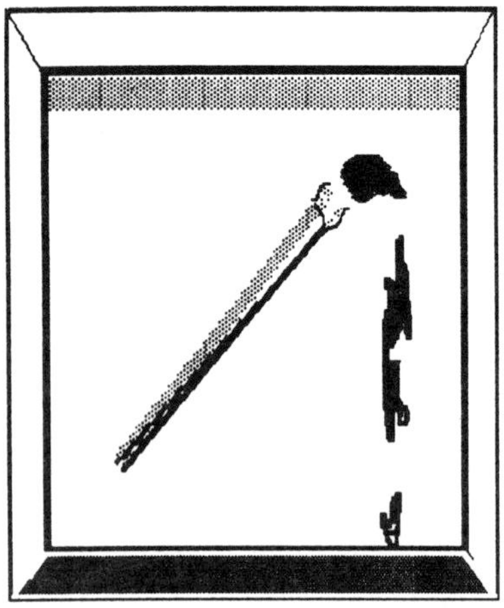

Have you ever heard the expression beauty is in the eye of the beholder? If two people look at the same object, one might think it is ugly while the other finds it beautiful. Perceptions (how we view or see things) differ. The illustration at the beginning of each biography represents the artist's perception of that person.

Directions: Study the illustration your teacher indicates and answer the questions below. Be prepared to discuss your responses. Then turn this sheet over and draw your version of the person or events depicted in the story. Include at least three things from the story in your picture.

1. What do you see?

____

____

2. What are the connections between the person depicted and the rest of the illustration? Explain.

____

____

3. What kind of mood is expressed and what does it mean?

____

____

4. Is the illustration historically correct? Now that you've read the biography, do you think the illustration represents the person well? Explain.

____

____

____

____

Acknowledgments

For permission to reprint all works in this volume by each of the following authors, grateful acknowledgment is made to the holders of coypright, publishers, or representatives named below.

Lesson 2, Handout 4
Exerpt from *The Wanderer: His Parables and His Sayings* by Kahlil Gibran. Copyright 1932 by Alfred A. Knopf, Inc., and renewed 1960 by Mary G. Gibran. Reprinted by permission of the publisher.

Lesson 2, Handout 5
Excerpts from *The Wisdom of Gibran: Aphorisms & Maxims,* Joseph Sheban, Editor. Published in 1966 by Philosophical Library, Inc., New York, New York.

Lesson 8, Handout 23
Excerpt from *Great Civilizations of Ancient Africa,* by Lester Brooks, 1971. Copyright by John Hawkins Associates, New York, New York.

Lesson 10, Handout 30
Map by Donna Sigisgalli. (c) 1989 by Chelsea House Publishers, a division of Main Line Book Co. Reprinted with permission.

Appendix, Handouts 54 and **55**
Two maps from *Maps: An Ancillary Program Support,* 1987. Published by D.C. Heath & Co., Lexington, Massachusetts. Reprinted with permission.

Appendix, Handouts 56 and **57**
Two maps taken from *Merrill Social Studies: Outline Map Resource Book,* 1986. Copyright by Merrill Publishing Co., Columbus, Ohio. Reprinted with permission.

THE PUBLISHER

All instructional materials identified by the TAP® (Teachers/Authors/Publishers) trademark are developed by a national network of approximately 300 experienced teachers whose collective educational experience distinguishes the publishing objective of The Center for Learning, a non-profit educational corporation founded in 1970.

Concentrating on values-related disciplines, the Center publishes humanities and religion curriculum units for use in public and private schools and other educational settings. Over 400 language arts, social studies, novel/drama, life issues, and faith publications are available.

While acutely aware of the challenges and uncertain solutions to growing educational problems, the Center is committed to quality curriculum development and to the expansion of learning opportunities for all students. Publications are regularly evaluated and updated to meet the changing and diverse needs of teachers and students. Teachers may offer suggestions for development of new publications or revisions of existing titles by contacting

The Center for Learning

Administrative/Editorial Office
21590 Center Ridge Road
Rocky River, Ohio, 44116
(216) 331-1404 • FAX (216) 331-5414

For a free catalog, containing order and price information, and a descriptive listing of titles, contact

The Center for Learning

Shipping/Customer Service
P.O. Box 910
Villa Maria, PA 16155
(412) 964-8083 • (800) 767-9090
FAX (412) 964-8992